BRIDGE ACROSS THE RIVERS

Partition Memories from the Two Punjabs

Edited by
Jasbir Jain and Tripti Jain

THORNBIRD
NIYOGI BOOKS

Published by

NIYOGI BOOKS

D-78, Okhla Industrial Area, Phase-I
New Delhi-110 020, INDIA
Tel: 91-11-26816301, 49327000
Fax: 91-11-26810483, 26813830
email: niyogibooks@gmail.com
website: www.niyogibooksindia.com

Editor: Mohua Mitra
Design: Nabanita Das

ISBN: 978-93-85285-73-8
Publication: 2017

Printed at: Niyogi Offset Pvt. Ltd., New Delhi, India

To the faith of those who build
bridges and cross over in friendship

CONTENTS

Partition, Dislocated Homes and Homelands

The Partition narrative is a complex web of political and religious discourse overlaid with diverse emotional experiences and responses. The literature it has generated also reflects these complexities and is an interplay of history and memory. The consciousness of the impending change, the threat to the oneness of a community, the fear of being uprooted and the need for flight were in themselves traumatic enough to have left a permanent mark. The frenzy of mob violence on one hand and the forced isolation of the individual on the other have all surfaced at some stage or the other in the narratives of the Partition. There is no way that emotional responses can be guided by the ruthless logic of political decisions.

The division of the country divided not only territory but everything that went with it—nation, homes and families. When freedom came in 1947, it also brought into existence a truncated India and gave birth to a new nation split into two wings. The fragile link between the two wings was later to be snapped with the birth of Bangladesh. The history of the period is one strewn with pre-Partition conflicts, violence and riots—all generated by the divisive policies of the long gestation period from the late nineteenth century to 1940 and after. The Lahore Resolution was passed in 1940 and was a clear call for division. Yet none fully grasped the full implications of the division—neither the political leaders nor the people. None visualised resistant borders, passports, visas and an aftermath of cyclical violence. Many felt that as soon as the trouble was over, they would return to their homes and resume life. Gyanendra Pandey points out that until 'almost the end of August 1947, Jinnah and Jawaharlal Nehru, along with a host of other leaders and officials on both sides, expressed their opposition to the transfer of populations…'(Pandey 41).[1]

In his work *Remembering Partition*, Pandey views the Partition as not one but three partitions: first, the Lahore Resolution 1940, second the splitting of the Muslim majority provinces of Punjab and Bengal, and third the massive exodus of the population and the rupture in the idea of a nation (Pandey 25-39). The dislocations and ruptures caused by the geographical relocations and emotional traumas find a place in the literature of the period and have continued to surface over and over again in different art mediums across the length and breadth of the country. The

---

1 Gyanendra Pandey in *Remembering Partition*, (Cambridge: Cambridge University Press, 2002), has given the history of the making of the Partition Autobiographics, memoirs and speeches provide details of the thinking that accompanied the conflictual interests of the different stakeholders. For more details refer Mushirul Hasan edited volume *India's Partition: Process, Strategies and Mobilization* (New Delhi: OUP, 1993), Asim Roy 'The High Politics of India's Partition: the Revisionist Perspective' *Modern Asian Studies*, 24:2 1990., Ayesha Jalal, *The Sole Spokesman: Jinnah, Muslim League, Indian Muslims and the Demand for Pakistan* (Cambridge, 1988), Ian Talbots, *Provincial Politics and the Pakistan Movement* (Karachi, 1988) and Joya Chatterjee 's *The Spoils of Partition: Bengal and India 1947-1967*, (New Delhi: Cambridge University Press, 2007.

impact is an ongoing one, though the nature of remembrance has not necessarily been static. In fact both history and memory are marked by inbuilt instabilities as both are contextual as well as accumulative discourses. New facts, documents and speeches help alter our perceptions as do the chronological shifts of the mysterious nature of 'recall'. How do we recall the past—through hearsay, oral history, experience or analysis? Or through its after-effects on our lives? Is it only a narrative of loss and thus of mourning, or does memory bring us some other recollections of community life and belonging? The past brings us a varied range of emotions and responses. The major body of the work that followed immediately after was experiential, autobiographical and a recording of personal anguish. These writings of first remembrance abound in the work of the Partition generation—Bhisham Sahni, Rajinder Singh Bedi, Khushwant Singh, Sadaat Hasan Manto, Mohinder Singh Sarna, Krishna Baldev Vaid, S.H. Vatsayan, Khwaja Ahmed Abbas, Gurmukh Singh Musafir, Qurratulain Hyder, Upendranath Ashk, Intizar Hussain are only some of them. Sahni's *Tamas* (1973) was later made into a powerful TV serial. It brought out the reality of religious politics very graphically through the use of a hireling to start a riot. It also brought home the tragedy of the long march across the newly-defined border. Manto's stories, short and cryptic, expose the mounting despair, the trauma of rape and the heartache as the insanity of a nation is expressed through Bishen Singh in *Toba Tek Singh*, where unable to understand the division, Bishen Singh martyrs himself on the border fence. Story after story unveils the darkness of the human heart in a world gone wrong. Vaid's *Guzra Hua Zamana* (1981) is a nostalgic account of the pre-Partition days. Vaid writes through the voice of his hero—a self-portrayal, 'What I really want now is to forget everything...that my mind is wiped clean…so that there is no desire to revenge…none of that' (334)[2].

Khushwant Singh's *Train to Pakistan* (1956) caught both the inter-community relationship and the play of power. It commented on the role of the British through the characters of the magistrate and the young prostitute. The latter also brought in the discourse of the homeless women who belonged to no definite territory, nation or religion. Bapsi Sidhwa, a Pakistani writer of the post-Partition generation has discussed similar issues in *Ice Candy Man* (1988). The fate of the abducted women and the nowhere land to which they belong has been analysed by Veena Das in 'The Anthrophology of Pain'. Das comments upon the silences that constitute an absent narrative of the women who have suffered:

> Human understanding gives way, language is struck dumb. A relapse into a dumb condition is not only a *sign* of the period but it is also part of the terror itself. It is this fact that violence annihilates language, that terror can be brought into the realm of the alterable which invites us to constitute the body as a mediating sign between the individual and society, and between past and present.[3]

In another chapter 'National Honour and Practical Kinship: Of Unwanted Women and Children', she comments on the whole process of bringing 'abducted women' back, at times, much against their will, with the unacceptability by their families staring them

---

2 K.B. Vaid, *Guzra Hua Zamana* (Hindi). Translated as *The Broken Mirror* (New Delhi: Penguin) 334, 334.

3 In *Critical Events: An Anthropological Perspective on Contemporary India* (New Delhi: OUP, 1995) 175-196, 184.

in the face. Where did these women belong? And their children—born or unborn? To whom did they and their children belong, which nation, which family and which land? This issue was discussed in several stories, films and historical analysis. Amrita Pritam's *Pinjar* (1950) later to be made into a film in 2003 and Jyotirmayee Devi's Bengali novel *Epar Ganga, Opar Ganga* translated as *The River Churning* (1995) record these tales of non-acceptability of women either abducted or compelled by circumstances to stay with friends from another religious community. The Hindi film *Chhalia* (1960) was one of the first films portraying this social ostracism of an abducted woman and *Gadar—Ek Prem Kahani* (2001), based on a real life happening, follows the same tragic narrative. In fact almost every anniversary of independence brings forth new recollections of the Partition or moves back into the past to introspect. Exiles and self-exiles, like Attia Hosain and other diasporic writers like Salman Rushdie, Anita Rau Badami and Shauna Singh Baldwin work through these memories. Social historians reassemble their findings—amongst them are Urvashi Butalia, Ritu Menon and Kamla Bhasin.[4] Mushiral Hasan's two-volume *India Partitioned: The Other Face of Freedom* brings together the narratives and reflections which were born during the crucial decade of the forties and provide a poignant description of the individual being caught up in difficult choices of an existential nature, choices of deep concern to their future. In Hasan's volume there is an extract from Josh Malihabadi's autobiography, *Yaadon Ki Baraat* (The Bridal Procession of Memories), wherein Josh reflects on the dilemma he faced with Nehru keen that he stay in India while his friends insisted that he move to Pakistan as the

4 See Butalia's *The Other Side of Silence* (New Delhi: Penguin, 1998) and Menon and Bhasin, *Borders and Boundaries: Women in India's Partition*, (New Brunswick, N. J., Rutgers University Press,1998).

relationship between the two countries deteriorated day by day. This was a move that tore him away from his familiar environment and landed him in the midst of a hostile reception.[5] Were these migrants citizens, exiles, refugees or muhajirs? It differed in each case. Manto never felt at home in Lahore.[6]

Attia Hosain's expression, she confessed, was stifled due to the absence of a 'family' to relate to. In a piece 'Voices of the Crossing', Hosain reflects upon the circumstances of her migration and her location in London in 1947. The fact that one of her brothers had moved to Pakistan was also responsible for her decision not to come back home to India to a divided family—a decision that turned her into an exile. She simply could not acquire a feeling of being-at-home in the country of her adoption. In another short piece 'Journey to No End' (*Wasafiri* No. 26) published in 1997, a few months before her death in January 1998, the reader is overpowered by the images of closure, of loneliness and coldness and the 'imprisoning building, darkness absorbed', the 'incisive cold entering each pore and probing inwards', 'no laughter, no terrace' and she continues 'Yet always I am going back through space and there is no way of stopping this scattering of myself for I have no guard against the sly abductors concealed and springing out from every vulnerable perceptive sense' (64). Attia Husain is, as once Mushirul Hasan wrote, of the 'heart-in-pieces' generation.

5 Malihabadi, 'My Ordeal as a Citizen of Pakistan' in *India Partitioned: The Other Face of Freedom*. EDd Mushirul Hasan,2 vols. Vol 2. (New Delhi: Roli Books, 1995), 200-207.

6 See the autobiographical essays and sketches on film personalities in *Bitter Fruit: The Very Best of Manto*. Ed. Khalid Hasan. (New Delhi; Penguin, 2008).

A similar sense of desolation pervades Intizar Husain's novel *Basti*[7] where the unnamed city is a ghost-town. The title translates as settlement, albeit a temporary one where an uncanny unrelatedness prevails. Memories travel, men travel but can cities and collectivities travel? *Basti* also draws attention to the graves where one's ancestors are buried and where, one day, it was assumed the living will be laid to rest. The question which resurfaces over and over again is not '*where* does one belong?' but '*how* does one belong?' Homes have been left behind and the new locale offers no acceptance. One longs to get back home even as fresh trouble breaks. Spanning both the partition of India and the partition of Pakistan, Husain's *Basti* is a narrative of the continued effects of the territorial and emotional division that was thrust on a population which really had no say in it with the power vested in the elite.

The Partition narrative exceeds the bounds of history, and it is the large scale exodus to which Pandey refers as the third partition, which was the most painful and the most long-lasting in its emotional, political and social contexts. It impacted both collective and individual identities. In some ways it rendered the individual invisible with identity being transformed into a stereotype which evoked conventional patterns of behaviour, and which in its turn flowed back into the social stream to constitute differences, conflicts, divisions and frustrated, failed individual lives. Manzoor Ehtesham's 1986 novel *Sookha Bargad* (New Delhi: Rajkamal Prakashan), where the banyan tree symbolised as nation is dead and no longer generates a cool shade. Similarly Munnawar Rana, a post-Partition child, in his long poem *Muhajirnama* writes about the heartache and anguish of divided families. Referring to the exodus he writes, '*Yeh*

7 Translated by Frances W. Pritchett (New Delhi: HarperCollins, 1995).

hijrat toh nahin thi, buzdili shayad hamari thi/Ke hum bistar pe ek hadi ka dhancha chod aaye hai ('This was not *hijrat* but perhaps our cowardice/on our way here we have left behind a skeleton of bones'.[8] In the introductory essay to the volume he attributes the strife in the Middle East to this rupture, thus tracing the ongoing impact of the partition on the Muslim identity, no matter where it is located.[9]

Rana's poem also problematises the role of recall, of how we see the past. Not having experienced it first hand, it ceases to be an isolated event, instead it envelops our present, affecting personal, community and cross-cultural relations. Histories of the past place events in a wider perspective and take account of intervening happenings which now constitute the aftermath and contribute to a reconstruction of the remembered past. These accounts of the past reflect the emotions of both guilt and compassion and form a counter-discourse to the recurring political conflicts and ideologies, reflecting the role of memory, which now distanced remembers differently. This long distance view is clearer and sharper and perhaps more honest, freed as it is from the fear and panic of the moment. It is what Hegel referred to as a 'thinking memory'.[10] More than official records, it is literature and the personal writings (such as memoirs and autobiographies) that take up the story of this memory, as the very notion of the real is placed under the scanner. If history has the 'other' outside the official records, memory has its 'other' embedded in the flow of time and often, a counter memory is generated, which

---

8 *Muhajirnama* (New Delhi: Vani Publishers) 35

9 '*Hum Khud Udharne Lagte Hain Turpei ki Tarah*', *Muhajirnama*, 9-29.

10 Refer Derrida, *Memoires for Paul de Man*. Translated by Cecile Lindsay, Jonathan Culler and Eduardo Cadava (New York: Columbia University Press, 1986.) Working through Hegelian terms, Derrida classifies memory as *Erinnerung* (interiorization) and *Gedachtnis* (thinking memory)

recalls the shared moments of happiness, the familiar and the known. It tries to grasp which is now placed outside its grasp.

Gyanendra Pandey in *Remembering Partition* also refers to two kinds of memory – of events and of responses – and observes that the two are present within the same discourse as two contradictory positions. 'First', he asks, 'how does "history" work to produce the "Truth" – say the violence of 1947 – and to deny its force at the same time' and second 'how can we write the moment of the struggle back into history?' It is this which leads him to conclude that the history of the Partition is neither singular nor static. It appears different from different perspectives (4-5). The past is never over, its presence looms large over our presents. Others like Alok Bhalla and Suvir Kaul, have pointed towards an ongoing responsibility of the present generation in how they read the Partition.[11]

Oral histories, however unreliable and selective, help in breaking up the hegemony of the written. Even as they are transcribed into script through an intervening mind, the story they narrate is as truthful as they believe it to be or have come to believe it as such. Urvashi Butalia, right at the beginning of her work *The Other Side of Silence*, acknowledges the uncertainty of the method and that memory is not ever pure or unmediated and asks 'How do we reach beyond the stories into the silence they hide?'[12] Ironically, it could also be the other way around, a telling which has escaped the censorship of politics and religion and is now free to explore itself.

---

11 Alok Bhalla ed. *Stories About the Partition of India*.(New Delhi; HarperCollins, 1994) xxxiii and Suvir Kaul, Introduction, *The Partitions of Memory* (New Delhi: Permanent Black, 2001), 13.

12 Butalia, (New Delhi: Penguin, 1998), 10-12.

Between 'official' history with its ongoing research and location in ideologies and nations on one hand and oral accounts on the other, are placed fictional narratives which offer psychological insights and a history of relationships. They move beyond facts and experiences to cultural constructs, the psychology of fear, and the uncertainty and bewilderment of the moment. Going beyond the moment they also move into its aftermath and, stepping outside collectivities enter individual psyches in order to explore questions of morality and ethics, of guilt and regret. A narrative creates a legible structure and shares a common ground with history. The experience of both – history and narrative – is of a sensibility, of entering the flow at the moment of crisis, of entering into an emotion and stepping into the psyche of the 'other'. Another thing which the two share is their journey to the past and a consciousness of time. Pandey has commented upon the shift in historical readings from the historical to the psychological, foregrounding the individual over the collective (11). He is cautious in his approach towards projecting Partition in any singular light. It is a multiple discourse which includes both: acts of brutality as well as of compassion. Betrayal when it comes is often motivated by self-preservation. The French philosopher Paul Ricoeur in his work *Time and Narrative* has pointed out that 'understanding the other people is the best analogue of historical understanding … ..the ability of one mind to transport itself into an alien psychic life on the basis of the signs that "express" – that is, make external – the intimate experience of the other person.'[13]

Yet, the retelling of a fictional narrative is very different from the retelling of history. While history, even in its shifts, has to adhere to its inner logical coherence, fiction is free to extract an incident or a 'truth'

13 Ricoeur, *Time and Narrative*, 3 volumes,(Translated by Kathleen Blamey and David Pellaur. Chicago: Chicago University Press, 1998), Vol 3, 148.

and shift both time and space. It invests the narrative with subjectivities and responses and makes visible the unseen or the unrecognised forces. Thus the truth it captures is real in an altogether different sense; it moves beyond statistics to emotions and consequences. When we turn to fiction, we do so both for the expression of pain and the turn towards healing. In between lie a whole range of emotions—of regret, guilt, loss, bereavement and mourning as well as the nostalgic remembrance of a lost past. Fictional narratives, in a measure, reflect upon those aspects of the experience which its immediacy is unable to capture as the mind struggles to understand it. But a temporal distance allows a re-entry into it. In fact, if one comes to think of it, the phrase, '*Itihaas sakshi hai*' (history stands witness) as Das observes, is a myth. History is enacted, it is in the process of happening, the agencies are multiple, and the logical explanations are half-truths. It is the human being who is a witness, and as she has argued in *Critical Events*, it is the woman's body that becomes a witness of these struggles as communities negotiate through violence (Das 56). One can also move beyond the gendered body to the 'self' whether child or adult, and to the moral conscience which is awakened only after suffering has been registered, when people realise that the Pakistani flag cannot be unfurled in India (Intizar Husain, 'An Unwritten Epic', Bhalla 633-657, that fields cannot be moved to another country, and the Taj Mahal is to be left behind. Men are mobile but the past is made up of deep-rooted associations. In *Aadha Gaon*, Reza tells the reader that the work is a narrative of belonging, 'This is my town, whenever I pass through its narrow lanes, it puts its hands on my shoulders. It meets me here and there on the roads of all my various stories.'[14]

---

14 Rahi Masoom Reza, *Aadha Gaon* (Hindi, New Delhi, Rajkamal Prakashan, 1966). Translated into English by GIllian Wright as *A Divided Village* (New Delhi: Penguin, 2003), 3.

The engagement with Partition is much more than a convenient incident to hang a plot on. It continues to concern us because similar divisionary politics and communal unrest continue to surround our lives, because the freedom struggle and the Partition are intimately woven into each other and also because despite cultural initiatives, relationships between the two countries continue to be antagonistic and every peace initiative is followed by a fresh eruption and consequent disruption of communication, trade and travel. The two contradictory discourses run parallel to each other as has been strikingly evident in the last quarter century: the people's will with its recognition of the human and the political aggression with its power politics.[15] Babri Masjid and the Gujarat genocide, the subsequent riots and community ghettos are all reminders of the wrong turns history has taken. The political fallout is evident in the politics of the whole world as violence overtakes all human values. It is imperative in such a time as the present to remind ourselves of the value of literary remembrance especially when it works towards producing a counter discourse to the narrative of history. It stands as a constant reminder of the existential values of life. In addition it is also symbolical of the voice of the people which politics refuses to hear.

In 2008, the Pakistani newspaper *Jung* and the Indian *Times of India* launched a project *Aman ki Asha*, (the hope for peace) directed towards bringing about greater understanding and facilitating cultural dialogues. Towards this end cultural exchanges and participation of writers, painters, theatre people, documentary makers and ordinary

---

15 See Rajni Kothari and Zia Mian, eds. *Bridging Partition: Peoples' Initiatives for Peace Between India and Pakistan*, (Hyderabad: Orient Black Swan, 2010) and Babar Ayaz's *What's Wrong with Pakistan?* (New Delhi: Hayhouse Publishers, Pvt. Ltd. 2013).

people—all have, at some time or the other, taken initiatives. It is evident that literature and art are indispensable means to the need to share and communicate because the two, strangely enough, express personal experience and also go much further than that. And the repeated return to history leads to an understanding of both the 'self' and the 'other'. It leads from an awareness of loss and guilt to a new sense of responsibility and reminds us that forgetting is no solution, instead one has to learn to remember and forgive and ask for forgiveness. Pandey explores the past in order to understand the role of memory and asks whether 'it is possible to recover a different kind of "national" past, recalling not suicide and murder ("sacrifice"and "war") and the eternally fixed collective subject, but labour and creativity and varied, internally differentiated communities, made up of a thinking, acting and changing human beings' (205). Painful memories often lead us to locate violence 'outside the village' (in a kind of anonymity) in order to preserve the community. Or perhaps, 'it is something more than guilt... that leads to such recollections and such forgetfulness' (see Pandey 177-183).

The Partition when it happened, threw up differences in its actual unfolding and in its impact on the two provinces—Punjab and Bengal. Debjani Sengupta in her introductory remarks to her anthology *Mapmaking: Partition Stories from two Bengals* (Manjul Publishing House 2011) has observed that Punjab has received more literary and political coverage than Bengal. One needs to look more closely at the history of the two provinces in order to grasp this difference. Joya Chatterjee in her work *The Spoils of Partition* has analysed the role of the *bhadralok* and in another article she has spelt it out even more clearly. She writes 'The migration out of East Bengal was very different from the rush of refugees into India from West Pakistan, which was immediate and immense, as was the way the dispossessed were received by the country, to which they fled. Unlike those from the west, the refugees from the east did not flood into India in one huge wave; they came sometimes in surges but often in barely perceptible trickles over five decades of Independence.'[16] The division in North India involved a larger area and the dimensions were different. It finally embraced NWFP, Sindh and half of Punjab and its influx and exodus both spread to Delhi. Vazira Zamindar in an account based on oral histories and newspaper accounts in both the countries has traced the recurring exodus of huge numbers often of the same people and the accompanying issue of permits, nationals and citizenships as well as the later issue of exclusively India-Pakistan passports introduced before their transformation to international passports[17] a part of our past, which with every fresh exploration reveals a new aspect. The coalition government in power at that time in Punjab, was not in favour of the division and Jinnah himself preferred collaboration, though, his hopes for a secular nation came to naught. Territories were defined and the country divided and identities both of 'nation' and individual stood at the crossroads. The negation of the idea of belonging was a complex one. Where did one belong, where was home? And how did one relate to a community in the process of rehabilitation? These were huge questions in themselves and had no easy solutions, else a complete overhauling of one's thought processes was required. A bewildered people on both sides of the border wondered how to negotiate the past and face an uncertain future.

---

16 Joya Chatterjee, 'Right or Charity? The Debate over Relief and Rehabilitation in West Bengal' in Suvir Kaul's *The Partitions of Memory*, 74-110, 74.

17 Vazira Fazila-Yaqoobali Zamindar, *The Long Partition and the Making of Modern South Asia: Refugees, Boundaries and Histories* (New Delhi: Penguin/ Viking, 2008,)

The present collection works with a chronology, located in time, first the immediate happenings and then recall and generational shifts. The seniority of writers has not been prioritised and in their placing the narratives gradually unfold a narrative of expectation, hope and harmony, its sudden disruption, flight and violence, psychological fallouts, rescue teams, gender issues and questions of guilt, belonging and reflection looking for some ways to relate. Over and over again they raise the question: how do we remember the past.

'The Homecoming' takes into its fold a migration in search of work and a bond of friendship between two men from different religions. The Muslim co-traveller stays with his Sikh friend in a gurudwara and faces no discrimination or ostracism. The longing for the homeland, for the families back home and the fields, now freed from mortgage, bind Mehtab Din and Sant Singh in friendship. The cultural past they share of rural Punjab is another connection. They chop wood in the gurudwara, ply hired rickshaws for a living as they wait for a passage home. The writer dwells on their loneliness and their dreams as much as on the economic and physical hardships they face. Amidst this, as the news of the community divide and hatred spread, suspicion and distrust make an entry, even in another country. Navtej Singh's story with its alternating discourse of hope and fear, of friendship under attack by environmental pressure goes on to emphasise both the oneness of mankind, irrespective of religion, as well as the pressures of political happenings on individual lives. The Punjabi title of 'Homecoming' is 'Desh Wapsi' which literally translates as 'Return to One's Country'. It marks the outward journey from a united homeland and a return to one on the verge of division. It also contains an ironical undertone bringing hope and despair in confrontation.

Sarna's story 'A Defender of Humanity', located in the months of the Partition exodus opens up another aspect of country/ homeland and nation. The Hindu and Sikh population is now in flight from their homes and fields and past associations. Several stories of exodus open up the whole range of border crossings: Lahore-Amritsar border, Firozpur border and in 'A Defender of Humanity', the Rawalpindi-Srinagar border. But as the tension mounts flight becomes more difficult. Unable to face the attacks by the tribals – the Kabaylis – the buses return to their base with their load of frightened passengers for whom it is nothing less than a sentence of death. It is amidst this atmosphere of fear and uncertainty that a Pathan driver stakes his own life to ferry his passengers across. When the tribal attack comes, he hands over the wheel to one of the passengers and borrowing a sword jumps out of the bus to an uncertain future. Like 'Homecoming', it is laced with religious references, which despite being particular are not partisan. A frightened Sikh passenger entrusts the Pathan to his 'Allah'. The sword is borrowed from a devout Sikh and becomes a symbol of Guru Gobind Singh's bravery. There is no way that the human can be denied, even if there is no way of holding violence back. The gradual building of the memory related to this flight which was full of fear being recollected by the writer several years after in the midst of his family in a town in India, are inevitably linked in survival, hope and faith, and perhaps gratitude.

Violence and survival were not the only two concerns—others were the difficult tasks of evacuation and rehabilitation. Can goodwill and harmony survive dislocation and terror? Is the human being resilient enough to cope with the aftermath? Kulwant Singh Virk's story 'Daughter's Dowry', works through the fear of death and forced conversions to an uneasy escape from hostile circumstances and comments upon the human ability to survive and plan for the future. It also comments on the importance of belonging to a community and the sharing of cultural practices. The refugee woman's walk becomes more confident when she has the two items meant for her daughter's dowry, firmly in her possession. But the reader is suddenly made to realise that the woman's mind is looking far into the future as the daughter is a mere child whose marriage is not likely to be celebrated for several years. Virk's other story which deals with a different aspect is 'Khabal: Perennial Grass'. The writer was a liaison officer at the time and this story is also about rescue operations. It brings in the additional problem of abduction even as it offers another comment on human ability to adapt to changed environments and the search for something to hold on to. An underlying subtext is one of possession in one and of silent sacrifice in the other. The sick woman's care for her sister-in- law is almost maternal.

Bhullar's 'Fattu the Bard' is the only story in this collection that expresses the experience of a return home after a migration – it works with two journeys – one to Pakistan and the other back to India, to his native village and to a house now totally razed to the ground. The nature of his rehabilitation is also different, as he has come back to a familiar homeland and the people he knows. True, it is also marked by the loss of a son and a daughter but his sense of belonging struggles to absorb these losses. Repeatedly it is stressed that 'belonging' makes a home. Human beings find it difficult to relocate in a new land, a new nation, especially when they are torn away forcibly. These realities are far more important than religious belief. The illogicality of the political demand is revealed at every step. The individual will has been bypassed in the whole process.

How little we know of the 'other', how slow we are to overcome prejudices is illustrated by Sarna's 'Of One Community'. In one case sacrifice and in the other the realisation of the shared trauma lead to an understanding of the 'Other', else we remain separated on account of prejudices, long persisting customs and social discrimination linking our lives to specific gods. Memory plays an important role in the above story, as it does in several others. In fact, memory is a significant part of belonging and of individual existence. It is also very selective in what it chooses to remember – a selectiveness which shapes our present – as it helps us to balance our perspectives. Baldev Singh's 'Come, Sister Fatima' is another very powerful story which has a strong sense of loyalty and commitment, one which allows Bebe to rise above differences, borders and time. Good neighbourliness, friendship and loyalty reign over all else and the old woman persists in holding on to her friend's spinning wheel placed in her custody, indifferent to the slim chances of ever restoring it ever to her. She may not even be alive! The generation gap surfaces in the difference of approach to the past as the mother and son carry on a silent war over the spinning wheel. The working of the spinning wheel after years of neglect is in itself a miracle carrying two different discourses—one as the symbol of freedom, of Gandhi and of self-sufficiency, the second of the Punjabi culture of the women folk and pastimes of an afternoon.

In several other stories there is an inevitable return to the past, seeking in it moments of shared happiness and belonging, moments the characters still hold precious. Surjit Sarna's two stories 'The Distance to Lahore' and 'A Bunch of Narcissus' are about the years 1946-47 and are a graphic portrayal of the creeping in of a sense of desolation on the city of Lahore as friends and lovers are pulled apart, as lives are dislocated, dreams die and flowers fade. The portrayal takes in its fold the closed educational institutions, the missing vendors and the absences of normal happiness. A counter portrayal is of the hectic activity of pamphleteering and the gatherings in the gurudwara. The writer's group of friends, the writers and artists of the period, the films and singers all come in for their rightful place in this nostalgic remembrance for it is relationships that build an atmosphere. 'A Bunch of Narcissus' is a narrative of disappointed love, unfulfilled aspirations and a romantic relationship cut short because it is an interfaith love. In the midst of this is the fragrance of the narcissus that keeps the association with the past alive even as the young woman is now a grandmother.

Ahmed Salim's 'The Man who Refused to Die' (original title 'Ishtaria', the one on police posters as a wanted offender) is about the constant presence of a cultural past which is too deeply ingrained to be affected by political change. It is another questioning of the construction of the concept of 'nation'. No nation ever existed on the strength of a single pillar. Languages, literatures and legends present a continuity which moves beyond all other variable temporary constructs and power dynamics. The young man engaged in reading Waris Shah's *Heer* is lost in a reverie where the long-dead author himself rises from the past. The political divide seeks to divide cultures but the legend and the legendary writer both defy all law. Salim's story is, in itself, a statement of the value of literature which captures reality perhaps better than history.

In 'Without a Homeland', Prem Parkash deconstructs the concept of belonging and enters the psychology of a refugee.. How does the individual relate to a homeland? A native hospitality, friendship, a sense of security, an at-homeness and continuity, supported by shared memories? The professor, however, has memories only of loss and suffering, of living in empty space and a deep sense of alienation.

The confrontation with his young tenant brings out the old man's bitterness. He points out that the other is equally homeless—where is the nation? And what, he asks, is patriotism? An empty abstract word or a tale full of blood and tears?

Conversion forms the background in several stories, as in 'Khabal/Perennial Grass,' 'You Shall Always be My World' and 'Gods on Trial' though each of the stories looks upon different issues and presents a different perspective. In Gulzar Singh Sandhu's 'Gods on Trial' the power of conversion as a measure of protection is questioned not only by the attack on the newly converted but also by the trial of faith. If there is a super power then faith is important, faith being the very basis of religion and it is this which is attacked through forced conversions. 'You Shall Always Be My World' is about true faith—the Sardar who wants the young boy to have a choice in the matter and the youth who resists conversion, even if it compels him to leave a familiar world behind and go towards an unknown future. Between them these stories work with escape, violence, courage and hospitality.

Daruwalla's 'Black Waters, Deep Well' moves in a different direction. Charting the whole course of school friendships, family backgrounds, old parents – from whom the truth has to be kept – Daruwalla goes on to paint a dark moment in the country's religious strife when young love is sacrificed. He moves from city to city, from farms to canals, to rivers providing details of the geographical map – the signposts of remembered experiences – as the impact of the Partition violence is fully felt. It too is a memory narrative as it crosses over from the present to the past and then back again. The lovers' death is not caused by partition violence, though it comes to be framed within it, but it is a tale of panic and fear caused by the commotion and the young couple is driven to death by water.

The last two narratives – Tahira Iqbal's 'One Own's Country' and Sanwal Dhami's 'Ointment' – are recollections of a past and of the role of time in this recollection. They voice similar pasts from two different geographical areas. Both work with fond memories of the pre-Partition years as well as the sense of loss of one's mother-country. And both happen to move across generations and work through patterns of guilt, regret, forgiveness and a longing for peace, a desire to reach across, to forget the past and to mend relationships. They are poignant in the heartache they make us share with them. There are several layers in the stories, layers of remembrance, regret, guilt and nostalgia. There is also a powerful urge towards peace and belonging, a need to rise above bitterness and hatred. They evoke similar memories and similar emotions in the reader.

The bridge that these narratives seek to build between 'self' and the 'other' is a bridge of understanding, a getting into the psyche of the other, and a realisation that suffering, loss and the aftermath have been on similar lines on both sides . It is also a bridge across rivers – the five rivers – which too have been a casualty of the Partition even as folklore still reflects them all: Ravi, Sutlej, Jhelum, Chenab and Beas. None of the two Punjabs can lay claim to all five. A bridge across the rivers is a necessary construct in order to move towards a freedom of the self and to liberate the 'human' held back by the 'difference' in religions and differently defined nationhoods. Perhaps memory and mourning together allow us to interpret the course of history anew and create understanding so that we are no longer chained by the past. Literature is one way of cohering affirmative memories one gathers in the course of understanding the pain and anguish of the 'other'. It opens a path for us to travel on so that the cycle of hate and revenge can be halted. Many of these stories are based on experiences and real life accounts, the fictional form is an artistic format. As the stories trace the shifts in emotions and focus on individual wills rather than politics, the undercurrents of cultural oneness form a counter discourse to aggressive politics. Almost seven decades have passed and it is time to intervene in the course of history and step out of negative emotions that continue to hold us captive. The present anthology is a collection of narratives that seek to debate issues and to throw light on discourses other than those of violence and darkness.

THE HOMECOMING

Navtej Singh

The third class in the launch was packed. Two British officers stood on the first-class deck, watching the chaos below.

"They're all going to Penang to catch the ship to India", one of them remarked.

"I wonder why they want to go back! They'll be cutting each other's throats the moment they land!" And the two laughed.

In the third class, Sant Singh pointed towards the West and said, "That is where our country is, behind those mountains."

Disembarking at Penang, Mehtab Din wondered where he would spend the night. Though he had only a small trunk as luggage, he still needed a roof above his head, because in Malaya, it could rain at any time.

Sant Singh loaded his luggage onto a Chinaman's rickshaw, and telling his wife to walk ahead, took his daughter in his arms. He had struck up acquaintance with Mehtab Din during their journey, and the two had discovered that they were from the same area in India and that their villages were only a few miles apart.

About to walk ahead, Sant Singh said, "All right brother, if we are lucky we may be able to travel in the same ship, and reach our villages together. Where are you staying here?"

"I am a complete stranger in this place and don't even know of an inn or *serai*. And perhaps, we may not have to stay long. The ship is sailing in a couple of days. I will spend the night on the verandah in front of a shop."

"Why didn't you tell me earlier? We are staying at the gurudwara, where they have very good arrangements for travellers. Come with us."

"Brother, will you not be troubled?" Mehtab Din asked hesitantly.

"It is the home of the Guru, how will I be troubled?" Sant Singh loaded Mehtab Din's luggage on to the rickshaw he had hired.

At the gurudwara the two stored their luggage in the same room. There was a big banyan tree in the large courtyard. Many travellers were staying there.

The two sat down on the platform under the tree. Some children were playing *gilli-danda*[1], and, on the other side, a few young men were singing *Heer*[2]. The singing of *Heer*, the game of *gilli-danda* and the sprawling Indian banyan filled Mehtab Din with deep nostalgia, and he felt he was back in his village.

---

1 Gilli-danda: An amateur sport – also called 'tip-cat' in English – played in the rural areas and small towns of Bangladesh, India, Nepal, Afghanistan and Pakistan as well as Cambodia, Turkey and Italy. Gilli-danda is an ancient sport of India, possibly with origins over 2500 years ago. The game is played with two sticks: a large one called a *danda*, which is used to hit a smaller one, the *gilli*. It is believed to be the origin of Western games such as cricket, baseball and softball.

2 *Heer*: It is one of several popular tragic romances of Punjab. There are several poetic narrations of the story, the most famous being *Heer* by Waris Shah written in 1766. It tells the story of the unfulfilled love of Heer and her lover Ranjha. Shah interprets the deeper meaning of the story as man's unrelenting quest for God.

Next morning the gurudwara was bustling with life. There was news that the ship to India would be in Penang within the next four days. Most of the travellers had come here after having wound up all their work, and some had been waiting for the ship for over two months. Many had lost hope, and were afraid that they would end up spending all their savings before they could go back, and probably have to seek work again on rubber plantations or shops. But the latest news had given them hope. The agent of the shipping company had come that morning and made a note of all those who wanted tickets.

Full of hope, some had even bought foodstuff and many were packed and ready for the journey. Women had already discussed the quantity of rotis to be prepared for the voyage. Mehtab Din and Sant Singh had also bought a *chulah* and some food. But when the ship sailed from Penang, only three of the travellers staying at the gurudwara had got tickets. All three were textile traders from Siam and had come to the gurudwara only a few days ago and had bought their tickets in the black market.

A pall of gloom fell on the gurudwara. The children did not play *gilli-danda*, and the young men did not sing *Heer*. An old man, sitting on the platform, remarked, "Why should we get tickets? They are only for these delicate sardars, who keep to their beds the whole day as though they have worms in their stomachs and are excreting money! At least this is what we have seen in these last few months."

In the morning, both, Mehtab Din and Sant Singh chopped wood for the langar – the free community meal service – at the gurudwara, and also filled water. When people had to be called to cook, even then, either one or the other would call for volunteers.

Mehtab kept his head covered the whole day, and would not let anyone enter bareheaded. They also helped in serving and were always the last to eat.

Mehtab would crumble the last roti and feed the pigeons that flocked in the courtyard in large numbers. One day, as he was busy scattering crumbs to the pigeons, he overheard an old woman telling the *bhai* of the gurudwara—"This maulvi is a good man."

"He is a man of God", answered the *bhai*.

A month passed and still there was no news about the arrival of the ship. They all ate at the *langar*, but the simple food was not sufficient. Sometimes, they bought some milk and a pinch of sugar to make tea, or would buy some pieces of bread and sweets for the little girl. Money had already been spent on buying food for the journey. Their savings were running low.

This was the real problem for if they ran out of their savings, the two would have to seek work. And what was more, they would need money even to travel back to their former places of work, perhaps only to find that their white bosses had already taken on other workers.

Mehtab was more worried because that morning he had received a letter from his brother, about their mother's death, asking him to come home on receipt of the letter. Mehtab remembered how his mother had always loved him more than his brother, and how, when he was leaving home for this island she had taken ill. She was almost blind and had broken down at his departure and cried, "A part of my body is breaking away to go across the seas."

However, it was necessary for Mehtab to leave home, even though he had not wanted to. The family was facing hard times. They had never been well off, but, his father had mortgaged a large part of their land in his lifetime.

Whatever land was left with them, had been flooded by the river. Mehtab had stopped his older brother from leaving home, and had told him—"You have no one here. It is a cruel land and those who go there seldom return. If I go, there are many forces to pull me back—my wife, my daughter. As soon as I have paid off the loan, I will return."

He had decided to earn as much as he could by hard labour and by living frugally. But the war had started soon after, and within days the island had been taken over by the Japanese. Mehtab had tried very hard to avoid conscription, but had finally been caught and put to work on laying the railroad.

He had survived the Japanese hell, and then found work in the tin quarries at three dollars a day. In the evening, he tended the cattle of a goods' carrier, and in return was given milk. Milk was very costly, so he used to sell that milk and earn some extra money.

Hard labour under the Japanese had aged him. His cheeks were sunken, there were dark circles under his eyes and wrinkles on his face. But he had finally paid off the mortgage.

With great pride, he had told Sant Singh—"I have been able to pay off the loan, by the grace of God, and the land that the river had swallowed has also been now reclaimed. I shall distribute two full cauldrons of rice to the community when I reach the village. They say that rice is very costly back home, but I shall keep my promise."

Mehtab was now desperate to reach home, but was compelled to stay on, for he could not buy a ticket in the 'black'. His hopes were gradually fading. Let alone two cauldrons of rice to feed the community, the money he had saved for his journey home was also fast disappearing.

One day Sant Singh's pocket was picked in the market. He lost about twenty dollars in this way, leaving both of them broken-hearted.

They rented two rickshaws to ply. The rental was five dollars per rickshaw, and whatever was left after this was theirs to keep. Not only was this a new type of work for them, but the plain food that they ate at the langar also weakened them. But fearing a shortfall in the money for their fares, they were reluctant to spend on extra food.

Whenever they saw a vendor pass by, they would stare at the food with hungry eyes. Sant Singh would sometimes say—"There is nothing to match the sweetness of the wheat of our country. Even plain roti is enough. Ever since I have come here, I have been surviving on this Australian wheat." If they passed a handcart loaded with American fruit, Mehtab would remark—"There is no fruit like the mango of our country."

For a few moments, rickshaws would be forgotten, and they would be transported to a mango orchard in their minds. The cuckoo would be spilling its heart out, and mother would be sitting near the *chulah* serving them hot rotis!

"Rickshaw...O rickshaw...rickshaw for two, and there is luggage also."

Rickshaws would again be running, jostling on the road, racing with speeding cars, trains and buses, winding through crowds.

Passengers were disembarking from a ship which had just come in from India. Mehtab's rickshaw was taken by two men and a child. He heard the beautiful child say—"Bapu, would there be any Muslims here? They did not even spare a child like me!" And the child began crying.

Two men, who were Muslims refused to take Sant Singh's rickshaw. He had not yet moved away, and he overheard one of them say, "'It is *haram* to give money to a Sikh or a Hindu. They have killed thousands of our brethren in Calcutta..." and the two boarded a Chinaman's rickshaw.

As Sant Singh and Mehtab Din sat sharing their experiences of the day, two Sikhs passed by. They had arrived that very day, and were staying at the gurudwara. They called Sant Singh and taking him aside talked to him. When he came back he looked upset.

"What were they saying?" Mehtab asked.

"No... nothing."

"Do tell me, why don't you?"

Catching Mehtab Din's hand and looking him in the eye, Sant Singh said, "They were saying that you are a Mussalman."

Surprised, Mehtab asked, "So what? Is this something new?"'

"They said that a Mussalman is like a snake... You may feed him all your life, but, one day he will surely bite you".

Mehtab sat as if turned to a stone, with downcast eyes. Sant Singh moved closer to him. "Silly! This is what they said. I told you because you insisted on knowing. But that is not what I believe. These people are mad. The real trouble-maker is the white man."

Meanwhile Bachno, Sant Singh's daughter, quietly settled down in Mehtab's lap. "Chacha, are you not going to feed the pigeons today? They have been waiting for you since long, poor things!"

Mehtab clasped her to his chest.

"Chacha, why are you crying? Your eyes are wet!"

"Why should I cry, my pigeon?" And Mehtab again clasped Bachno to his chest. Bachno wrapped her small arms around his neck. Sant Singh looked with warm affection in his eyes.

Finally, all the travellers staying at the gurudwara got their passage, and the ship was leaving the next day.

Handing in their rickshaws, they counted the money they had saved. They were happy for after taking into account all the expenses, they would still have some money left. Taking Bachno with them, they went shopping. Sant Singh bought a beautiful pair of shoes for Bachno, and a length of Chinese silk for his wife. Mehtab also bought a length of the same material for his wife. He also bought a pair of shoes for his daughter Tajo. She was Bachno's age and the same size would fit her.

The sea was stormy and many travellers were seasick. The next day things were worse with huge waves spilling over the decks.

That day Bachno took ill. Both Sant Singh and his wife had been seasick since the second day itself. Only Mehtab was well and he took care of Bachno, holding her to save her from the waves that washed over the deck and cleaning up after she threw up.

Many a time, he felt that it was Tajo in his arms. He had often called his little Tajo a pigeon; and by now she would be as big as Bachno. She would not know him, for she had been very small when he had left home. When he slipped her new shoes onto her fair feet – she had her mother's fair complexion – she would strut about the village, showing off before all the children of the village. And her mother would tell her—"Tajo, this is your abba." Her mother would herself be delighted with her Chinese silk suit. Such cool silk! When he had left home, with tears in her eyes she had told him—"Don't stay on there, I beg of you, for my sake, for Tajo's sake." And now, he was keeping his promise to her, and going back. She would still be young—the same as she had been earlier, with *surma* in her eyes, and her fair body. Suddenly he put his hand on his face; stubble scraped his fingers, and the dark circles under his eyes hurt him....

A very high swell rode over the railing and flooded the deck.

The ship was delayed by the storm at sea, and docked at Calcutta two days later. The city was already in the grip of riots and Sant Singh with his family and Mehtab Din caught the train to the north that very night.

The train journey was as difficult as the one by sea. The distance to be covered was long; but they were not agitated, as this was their own country. They bought mangoes, and ate some during the journey. The rest they put away to take home. Bachno had been born in Malaya, and this was her first visit to her own country. Her first taste of a mango! She told Mehtab – "Chacha our own country is very good, as good as you said it was!"

Mehtab planted a kiss on her forehead! The tangy smell of the mangoes was encircled her.

A strange happiness tugged at Mehtab's heart at the thought that Tajo too would find these mangoes sweet, as also her mother, and they would also exude the same tangy fragrance around them.

The train ultimately reached its destination, the terminal where they were to get off. They found the atmosphere at the railway station strange and tense.

Sikhs and Hindus were seated in a group and the Muslims in another. The police was all over the station, Mehtab and Sant Singh had never seen so many policemen. They also noticed that even the beggars were careful as to whom they begged from, selecting their targets on basis of religion.

Coming out of the railway station, Sant Singh beckoned to a tongawala. A Sikh tongawala came forward.

"We have to go to the bus stop, brother. Three adults and one child. How much will it be?" Sant Singh asked.

Glancing at Mehtab, the tongawala asked—"Is he Muslim?"

"Yes."

"Don't take him with you. The route that I will take is not safe for him. You are welcome."

By this time, a Muslim tongawala had come to Mehtab and asked—"Want to go to the bus stop? You come with me. The Sardar will pass through the Hindu areas. I will take the route through Muslim mohallas; though it is circuitous it is safer!"

Bachno started crying—"Chacha, where are you going? You told me that you would take me to Tajo and she and I would be best friends!"

The Sikh tongawala had set off, with Bachno still calling out to her Mehtab chacha!

Although his tongawala took the longer route, yet Mehtab was the first to reach the bus stop. He bought the tickets, and put in his luggage and reserved the seats for them all, and then looked around. There was a grain shop right opposite the bus stop. He decided to find out the price of rice because he had to fulfill his vow of feeding the community. But he found that the shopkeeper said nothing, merely shook his head to indicate that there was no rice.

He climbed into the bus and sat down. Tajo and her mother were no longer at an ocean's distance from him. He had paid off the loan. Now, life would be more comfortable. The river had also given up the land it had swallowed: now reclaimed, it was more fertile than before. People were saying that India would soon become independent. The white man would leave soon.

It was getting late, but Sant Singh's tonga had not yet arrived. The bus driver told him that he would be leaving in an hour. Though there was still time, Mehtab decided to walk up to the main road to look out for them.

As he reached the main road, he heard a loud blast further up near the crossing. He also saw a tonga lying on its side on the road. The road was deserted. Fear clutching at his heart, he quickly walked up to the tonga. He saw the bodies of Sant Singh and his wife on the ground, badly ripped apart and slashed.

Sant Singh's legs lay at some distance from his body; an iron rod in his wife's breast was soaked in blood.

Unconscious Bachno lay at a distance with blood on her forehead, and arms, which were badly slashed. Mehtab rushed forward to pick her up in his arms. Her body was still warm and she was breathing.

Mehtab set off with rapid steps. His tears fell on the little girl who had lost both her parents, coming to her country for the first time. Mehtab recalled the time they had spent together waiting for the ship, plying rickshaws, and how Sant Singh had longed for a taste of the wheat of his country.

Bachno's mother had yet to get her new silk suit stitched. They had eagerly soaked in the sights and smells of their country. A short while ago they had been full of hopes and expectations. Now, only Bachno was left...the only living thing... in this land of death...he would not let her die, never.

"Bachno, this is Mehtab. I will look after you like my own Tajo. You will not be just good friends; you will be sisters!" Mehtab was calling to Bachno.

Perhaps, she heard him. Her eyelids fluttered—"Chacha...you."

Suddenly, Mehtab was stabbed in the back. The unconscious Bachno fell from his arms.

"Kill this little snake also", the dying Mehtab heard, and then the scream of a child.

In great pain, Mehtab stretched his arms towards Bachno, but she was too far away.

"Bachno...Tajo..." and his lifeless arms fell to the ground.

Like the howling of the village dogs before a death, the siren for curfew was blaring full blast. There was no one on the road except for the white soldiers.

Translation: Tripti Jain

A DEFENDER OF HUMANITY

Mohinder Singh Sarna

Today I thought of you again. I always remember you this way, all of a sudden. And I remember you often. And always when the sun is shining brightly on my life, chasing away the shadows. When the valley of my life is wreathed in smiles, when sunflowers are blooming, when my son comes back victorious from some debate competition, when my daughter creates a new ikebana design, when my wife puts a plate of my favourite pea *pulao* in front of me, wipes her hands on the end of her sari and smiles at me, I remember you all of a sudden, with all my heart.

That was how it happened today too. My daughter was narrating jokes and we were all doubled up in laughter. She's got an endless store of jokes. Doctor jokes, lawyer jokes, husband-wife jokes, priest jokes, truck-driver jokes. Today she was telling truck-driver jokes when all of a sudden my eyes filled up with tears and I left the lawn and withdrew to my room. I could hear my daughter's voice coming after me.

"I bet Papa has gone in to write a story."

I hadn't left the lawn to write a story. But my daughter's words stirred the memory of your story inside me. Why not write your story today? The story that has been stoking your memory in my mind these last thirty-six years!

That cloudy morning of September 1947 is fresh in my memory, the morning when all of us climbed into your lorry. You were in the driver's seat, looking intently into the mirror to straighten the Pathan turban that you had tied over the little black cap on your head.

Outside the lorry it was all mist and cloud. Inside there was utter terror. The passengers sat, huddled into themselves, their hearts in their hands. Even in this atmosphere of fear I was transfixed by your fine features, your handsome face. Centuries of mingling of Pathani, Pothohari, Greek and Afghan beauty that had been taking place in north-west India seemed to have reached its apogee in your face.

Suddenly one of the passengers exclaimed, "Look, the previous lorry has returned."

We all turned to look. The lorry that had left at six in the morning from Rawalpindi for Srinagar had indeed returned. Its passengers, frozen with fear, unable to speak. But its Muslim driver was relating, with extravagant gestures, how the tribals had reached the road that ran from Rawalpindi to Srinagar, how they had fired upon the lorry near Ghorhagalli and tried to puncture its tyres, how he had not lost his nerves but had brought the passengers back to safety by driving the lorry in reverse gear for nearly six furlongs.

There was no joy on the faces of the passengers who had been brought back to safety. They knew that the death they had escaped now awaited them here. All the routes for getting out of Rawalpindi to India had been cut off. Train-loads of passengers were being massacred even before they got to Jhelum or Wazirabad. In the last ten days not a single train had managed to pass Lahore and reach Amritsar safely, and now there were no trains at all. There had been some hope of escaping by road towards Srinagar. This hope too had now been strangled by the tribal raiders. The stabbing incidents in Rawalpindi itself were on the rise and one by one they would all be killed. Not a shred of hope left.

At that moment you turned back and looked at your passengers, saw their distress, read the intense hopelessness in their eyes and took a measure of the terror that gripped their souls. I saw a dark glint appear in your fearless eyes. Thumping your chest you said: "I will take you to Srinagar, even if I have to stake my life on it. Are your ready to go?"

Such courage coming from a Muslim driver couldn't but touch the hearts of the Hindu and Sikh passengers. They were ready to go; in any case, they had no other choice.

The driver of the first lorry pleaded, "Don't go Hussain. Think of yourself: you have an old mother, an unwed sister."

But you paid him no heed and pressed your foot firmly down on the accelerator.

Nurpur, Kohmurree, Nathiawali, Ghorhagalli passed without incident. Kohalla was twenty-five miles from Ghorhagalli. At Kohalla there was a bridge across the Jhelum river. On this side of the bridge the new country of Pakistan ended, and on the other side the territory of Kashmir state began. It was downhill all the way from Ghorhagalli to Kohalla and the lorry had picked up speed. But the passengers were still afraid. Would they ever cross that bridge to breathe free in the India of Gandhi and Nehru, or would their bodies be picked to the bone by vultures on these rough hilly slopes under a merciless sky? Holding their breath, they watched each passing milestone. Now Kohalla was seventeen miles away.

Suddenly we heard gunfire and saw blood spurting from your left arm. Behind me sat Pritam Singh Sodhi who was a compounder and used to volunteer at the Rawalpindi Singh Sabha's charitable hospital. He jumped to his feet. Your wound wasn't deep. The bullet had gouged a gash through your muscle and gone out of the lorry's window. Pritam Singh Sodhi took out the first-aid kit from his suitcase and bandaged you. Even as he was ministering to you, you didn't let the lorry's speed slacken one bit. You had lost a lot of blood but your face was still flushed with determination and the black glint in your fearless eyes had not dimmed a whit.

We heard the sound of gunshots again when we were only twelve miles from Kohalla. We looked in all directions. Twenty yards behind us stood four young tribal men, their rifles aimed at the lorry's tyres.

"Is there a driver amongst you?" you asked, without taking your eyes off the road. "If so, then he should come up here fast."

Jodh Singh spoke up: "I've been driving buses for the Nanda Bus Service from Pindi to Lahore. But I don't have any experience on hilly roads."

"Hold the steering wheel," you said. "It's downhill all the way to Kohalla. Keep your foot on the brake. And for the sake of your Guru, don't stop the lorry this side of Kohalla."

And you stepped up to Sardar Shamsher Singh and requested, "Sardar ji please give me your sword."

Without understanding but without a minute's hesitation, Sardar Shamsher Singh handed you his three-foot-long sword. You unsheathed it and jumped off the moving lorry, saying "God be with you." We saw you roll into the bushes and then swerve off into a bunch of trees. In your hand was the gleaming sword that Guru

Gobind Singh had put into the hands of the Khalsa to protect the weak. It looked beautiful in your hand because it was the sword of humanity and you were the defender of humanity.

Three more bullets were fired but they didn't touch the tyres. Then the bullets stopped. We could see that your gleaming sword had caused pandemonium among those young tribals.

I don't know what happened to you. You were one against four. And who knows how many more were hiding in the trees. And they had rifles.

When you jumped out of the moving lorry, I sent up a prayer: "May Allah protect you, Hussain. May he grant you the remaining lifespan of cowards like me."

I do not know if He heard my prayer or whether they finished you off. What happened to your mother, what became of your sister… that too, I do not know.

But I remember you often, and always in the happy moments of my life. This life and its joys are your gift to me. That is why when your memory knocks at my door, a hundred prayers burst forth from my heart. I hope to God that you are still alive. But if you're not, I hope that Allah has given you a place in heaven. Wherever you may be, through this story today I send you my salutation, the salutation of my wife, son, daughter, and of all humanity.

Translation: Navtej Sarna

DAUGHTER'S DOWRY

Kulwant Singh Virk

It was 1947. The situation in West Punjab was dominated by the Muslims. This made things very difficult for poor Allah Rakha. Allah Rakha was not a Muslim by birth. He had accepted Islam to save his life. When many of his neighbours were killed in the riots, he had then begged to be converted to Islam. He had been given the name of Allah Rakha, because had Allah not protected him, he too would have been killed.

Though his life had been spared, it was difficult for him to save himself. He was like a cornered doe, full of fear. Where could he go? It seemed to him that all men, houses, walls and roads were his enemies. He was like a man walking on burning hot coals, shaky and infirm. The town was full of people, but he could not share his feelings with anyone. Some men were good and some bad, but there was none he could call his own. He disliked everything, the new food he ate, his new clothes, his face as it was now, and his new companions. It was he and his wife. They would sit and try to figure out ways and means to escape from the situation into which they were. They were even afraid of their children that they might inadvertently reveal something overheard at home.

At that time I was in Pakistan, and had the responsibility of locating such families and help them reach India. One day, he saw me and signalled to me to move to a corner. I did, but he did not join me. He was frightened of even being seen to be talking to me, and was apprehensive of being shot, as he stood talking to me. He met me again after two days, and wanted to know where he could meet me after three hours. I told him that he could come to my residence. His intentions were clear. He wanted to go to India. He did come to my bungalow after three hours. We left for his home in a truck, along with some soldiers.

The people of his *mohalla* were greatly annoyed when they saw him with me. It was easy to understand the meaning of my presence by his side at that time—that he was leaving Pakistan for India. For them it was a betrayal. After all, Allah Rakha was one of a small group of persons who had been spared because of their uprightness. They had not spared his life to have him leave Pakistan, after a few days, riding in the safety of a military truck. He was, in this manner, insulting their faith in him by switching sides. Allah Rakha was also frightened by the anger so clearly evident on their faces. His fear had now become a habit, and my truck did not give him a powerful mantra to rid him of this fear.

The lane to his home was very narrow, and the truck could not be taken in. We had to park on the road and walk through the lane to his home. His wife was there, greatly frightened. I could not properly gauge the extent of her fear. I had not experienced what she had—human life being totally devalued. She was afraid of being turned into a corpse like the ones she had seen strewn on the roads and in the bazaars a few months back. When she saw me, she seemed to recover some courage. Their luggage was already packed, and they were ready to leave. We waited for their daughter to return from school, who came in a few moments later.

"*Salaam-u-laikum,*" she said in the manner she had been taught at school. "No, girl, say *Sat Sri Akal*. We are going to India now. Allah Rakha's wife gave her the good news, picking her up in her arms. Then, she looked straight ahead, as if trying to peer into the unknown future, and said. "We will arrange your marriage there."

The news that Allah Rakha was leaving spread rapidly through the neighbourhood, and people began collecting to see him leave. Some stood against the wall of the lane, and others mounted the wall. Many were peering from over the wall, and a few watched from their roofs or balconies of their homes. Some of those standing in the lane had rifles and the belts slung across their shoulders with glistening bullets. What was the use of having a rifle, if it was not to be displayed on such an occasion? The atmosphere was charged and fearful.

The luggage had to be loaded, and there was no question of any help from any quarter. Were I to help, it would not only tarnish my standing as an officer but also demean me in the eyes of the assembled crowd. If the soldiers were to help, it would have jeopardised all our lives. Thus, there was only Allah Rakha to do all that work. The mattresses and quilts had already been bundled, and the utensils were tied up in sacks. There were also a couple of trunks. As Allah Rakha loaded the luggage, the anger of the crowd was mounting. Sometimes they were squabbling between themselves—"You had been told to finish him off! Now look!" One man was complaining bitterly.

"*Oye*, we will finish him now. What's the problem?' Another from the crowd answered.

Even I was getting frightened by the hostility around us. The lane was narrow and full of places to hide and anyone could fire at us from any point. We would not be able to escape because that would incite them all the more, and there was a danger of things getting out of control. But, finally all the luggage had been put in the truck and in the last round I had brought his wife as well. In my opinion we had time enough to leave immediately before things got worse.

Before getting into the truck, Allah Rakha's wife looked at the things in the truck. A few things were missing.

"You have not brought that large metal pitcher and the kettle?"

"What were they tied in?"

"They were not packed, but placed near the pillar."

"They cannot be brought now. Where so much has been left and the house as well, let them also be. Come get in and lets go."

Allah Rakha was right, It was dangerous to fetch them. The crowd's anger was at its peak because we were now about to leave. They were abusing us, and there was a danger of violence or even shooting at any moment. It was also possible that some of them had already entered his house in order to loot, and if anyone was to go back there could be trouble. But, these arguments did not have any effect on Allah Rakha's wife. She was intent on getting those things.

"They must be fetched," she said looking at her daughter, and then at the few things stowed in the truck. She walked back to the house all alone.

I also went after her because my presence had a dampening effect on the simmering tempers. Tucking the large metal pitcher under one arm, she picked up the kettle in the other hand.

"Where would you keep lugging them around? They are so heavy," I gave her a mild scolding.

"What if they are heavy? What would I give my daughter in her dowry?"

As we walked back, her strides were confident and strong. Her determination had an effect on the crowd which stood around. Getting into the truck, she gathered up her daughter in her arms and sat down on one trunk, and spread one leg on the pitcher and the other on the kettle.

Translation: Tripti Jain

KHABAL ~ PERENNIAL GRASS

Kulwant Singh Virk

This is a story of Pakistan.

Pakistan had just come into existence, barely three or four months ago. Things here were still in turmoil. Police stations were overcrowded with all kinds of articles. Trunks, bedsteads, cradles, tables, sofa-sets, pictures…all had abandoned their original positions and moved to the police stations. Else, what need of cradles and pictures at a police station? These things must have occupied a special place in their own homes. At that time, their owners must have thought that they would not fit into any other space except the one that had been assigned to them. But, at present, they were lying scattered all over in heaps. Utensils, cupboards had been displaced from rooms and kitchens, and were now piled up in front of government offices. No one had cleaned or polished them, and nor even counted them. Months had passed since a human hand had touched them.

Things were in a flux in Pakistan. Many animals, uprooted from their own mangers and sheds, now wandered around, looking at things with bewildered eyes, frightened of the new places they had strayed to. In all this turbulence, the only thing that stood firm and rooted in its place was the earth.... Numerous refugees, displaced and without roots wandered all over. They would be sent ahead from the large base camp at Wagah, and then, moved from district to district, village to village, in carts or on foot, in search of land.

Not only refugees, but even the old residents had been dislocated. Communities were broken as various members had moved away, and friends had lost friends. The workers in the mills had lost their owners, and the millowners had no labour. New people had come in their place. These new people were strange and dirty, and somewhat bewildered. They did not mix with the old residents. They did not sit down near you to begin a conversation after "*Salamu laikum*", but would stand at the door and keep peering in. If you asked them in, even then, they would not move. These people had shaken the foundations of the villages. The villages seemed unfamiliar even to those who had lived here all their lives, because now they were no longer what they had been earlier. Even the canals and their channels flowing near their *havelis* seemed unfamiliar. They did not perform their *wuzoos*, the ablutions for the prayers, with these waters anymore. For days, the waters flowing down these canals had been red, and many corpses and mutilated bodies had come floating down them. How could one use this water for *wuzoo* now? They stopped even unknown strangers from bathing in these waters. Actually, everything was in a turmoil, and making an intense effort to come back to normalcy. Everything was trying to go back to its original place, to plant its feet firmly on the ground. Everything cried out for restoration. One young Jat, having surveyed the ruin that lay around, commented to his father—"The country has been ruined."

"It does seem like that, but let's see what turn events take. If things settle down then everything should be fine."

"All that is only talk; how on earth will these poor people settle down? They are not capable of even putting a morsel in their mouths."

"Oh, no, silly. It only looks like that. Look, at those fields, you see that *khabal,* that perennial grass in those fields? When we till the land, do we leave it there? We pull it out, root by root, and throw it away. But, ten days later, you will find it sprouting in the field, and within a month it looks as if the field had never been ploughed."

There seemed to be an element of truth in the old man's statement. People who were given land seemed to settle down, even if the lands were allotted to them only on a temporary basis. This seemed to raise their spirits. They dug up small pits near their newly made sheds and lit fires of cow-dung cakes, and sat around with hookahs and liquor. Gradually, their buffaloes also settled down in their new sheds. They scratched their skins under the horns with the branches of trees, hanging over the sheds, and sometimes even used the walls of the sheds to scratch their backs in sheer abandon. Whenever the tehsildar or any other official visited their new village, then, many of them would try to assume the role of a *panch*. They would tell the tehsildar about the general problems faced by the villagers in such a way as to demonstrate that they represented the village, and, in this manner, assert their leadership. They would make all the others sit at the back and tell them, "only one should speak", and, by offering the officer refreshments, try to become the focus of his attention. All these things proved that this setback had not dampened their spirits.

In this uprooted-settling-down Pakistan, I was appointed the liaison officer by the Indian Government.

My responsibility was to look for the women who had been abducted and forcibly converted to Islam, and restore them to their families in India. I had a special troop of Indian army and special police of Pakistan to help me.

The work of locating lost girls was, both easier and more difficult than looking for other lost things. Sometimes, a girl could be found after a little effort, and, at times a girl simply could not be found despite many attempts. The Pakistan police did help a little in persuading, them – this they called 'recovery'– but, rarely gave any information on their own. Even then, when they really wanted to, they made the task of recovery easy.

The incident I am talking about concerned an abducted woman. To locate her not only did the police inspector of that area accompany me, but, it was he who had actually given me the information about her. He also told me that the woman was the daughter-in-law of the *nambardar*[1] of a village in his area. The village we had to go to was in a remote area, far from the road. We spent a long time travelling through the lanes on foot.

When we reached the village, the *chowdharys*[2] of that village gathered to welcome the police. At that time, the government in Pakistan was held in great awe. When the *thanedar*[3] asked about the woman, they immediately pointed towards a house. This small house was at one corner of a large compound. The *thanedar* stayed

---

1 Nambardar: Title in India and Pakistan applying to powerful feudal families of zamindars of the village or town, a state-privileged status which is hereditary and has wide ranging governmental powers: the policing authority of the village, and many other governmental and administrative perks

2 Chowdhary: Head of clans and castes in a village, wielding considerable power over administrative matters

3 Thanedar: A police constable

behind, and I went in alone. It was a small mud house. On one side there were a few glasses and *katori*s and *thali*s on a wooden rack. A couple of mattresses and a few other articles lay heaped in another corner.

The woman was lying on a cot. She seemed to be ill. One hand and arm were bandaged. Perhaps, there had been a fight. She looked dispirited and broken and spoke in a low voice. I sat down on the cot next to hers.

"What is the matter with you?" I asked her a simple and straight question.

"I have been running a fever the last few days."

"Is there no other woman here with you?"

"No, no one else is here."

Her situation was unlike the situation of abducted girls and women I had met earlier. They had been surrounded by men and women, and had been watched all the time by someone or the other when I had met them.

This woman was living all alone in this house, as though her abductors had abandoned her to her fate. It also seemed that these people had helped her. I had also been told earlier how her whole family had been killed. I did not want to hear it from her a second time. I was more interested in her present situation.

"How long have you been living here?"

"Since the village was ransacked."

"Who gave you these utensils and clothes?"

"You have lost your mind!"

I understood what she meant. She was not living alone, and the articles and clothes lying here were not her own. Only, the owner of this house, articles and her body, was nowhere to be seen.

I have written these facts very easily, but, at that time, this information came as a big shock to me. All the good thoughts and feelings I had been entertaining about the police helping the people and about the world at large vanished in a moment. I confronted the hard reality of the situation. Here lay the abducted wife of someone, dispirited and broken, on a cot in this mud house. The ugly picture of cruelty of man to man was before my eyes.

Humiliated and trampled, she lay here—ill with fever. No one from her caste, community, village or religion was with her. No one had told her that she could still meet her lost family. Had anyone else told her she would have refused to believe it. After all, who could take her out of this big powerful Pakistan, and how? It was futile even to think of this possibility.

There was no question of taking her away immediately. It was midwinter, and it was not advisable to relocate her in her condition. These people could not whisk her away, because we had seen her with our own eyes, and they were all fully aware of the consequences.

"All right, bibi, I'll be back another time." By saying this that "I will be back," I meant that I would take her away from here, but perhaps, she could not even dream of this possibility.

"Are you leaving now? Sit down for a moment, and listen to something that I have to tell you."

I again sat down on the cot next to hers.

"I have some work for you. I beg you, implore you to do this much for me."

"What is it?"

"You are my Sikh brother. I was also once a Sikh. Now, I am a Muslim. There is no one I can call mine in this world. I am in great difficulty. Please hold my arm. I have a young sister-in-law, my husband's sister. The people from Chak 11– may they perish– have taken her, that day these people had made the biggest attack on the village. You appear to be a person of importance. Please bring her to me. They all defer to you, even the police listen to you. Implore them to give her back. I have brought her up like a mother. She will come to me. I would arrange her wedding myself and marry her off to someone. There would be someone with me. I'll be able to call someone my own."

The old Jat's statement came to my mind—"Look there, there, at that perennial grass in the field. We had spared no effort in rooting it out, had pulled it out by root and thrown it away. But, after ten days, you can see it sprouting all over."

Translation: Tripti Jain

GODS ON TRIAL

Gulzar Singh Sandhu

Noora sat quietly under a mango tree by the tombs of the pirs. He was absorbed in doing the home task given by his teacher. Rahmte, his sister, was cutting fodder from the Sikh Martyrs' field, near the pirs' graveyard.

The Martyrs, entombed near our field are supposed to possess miraculous powers transcending death, fire and time. We of the Sikh religion have profound faith in them. So much so that I was not allowed even to sit for a school exam unless I pledged an offering to them. My grandfather believed that it was only because of the Martyr's kind intercession that I had never failed in any examination.

That summer day, I too was with Noora under the mango tree. While Noora was engrossed in homework I watched Rahmte, cutting fodder from our field. I liked her so much that I felt like talking about her to Noora.

"Of your two sisters whom do you like more? Rahmte or Jaina?" I asked.

"Jaina," he said, naming the elder one that had been married for four years then.

"Why don't you like Rahmte" said I and was suddenly aware that I could be misunderstood.

"She beat me once, which Jaina never did", he said casually and to my satisfaction and returned to his book. Assured that I was not misunderstood, I started watching the rhythmic movement of Rahmte's limbs operating the sickle.

Just then something startled a peacock on the Martyrs' peepul tree, and it shot off into the air flapping its large wings with a heavy, muffled thud-thud. One of the feathers came off and sailed down to the ground. I was then a keen collector of peacock feathers. As I saw one sailing down in its rich dazzling colours, I threw down my book and ran for it. But it never touched the ground. Rahmte had grabbed it from the air before I could.

"Hand it to me," I said a little tersely.

"I got it first,"she replied coldly.

"None of that!' I threatened. "You have to give it to me."

"Oh, I have to, have I?" she scoffed. "In that case I shan't!"

"Come on, hand it over and I'll never ask for anything else from you." I tried to sound suggestive and grown up. She flushed.

"Take it, there," she said curtly throwing the feather away. She collected the fodder into a sheaf, picked it up and started home. I could not take my eyes from her slender figure, straining under the weight of the sheaf. I was left wondering whether I had really offended her.

Back in the graveyard I found Noora's father the saintly Badru, saying his namaaz. Noora stood by humbly. Both the father and the son had incongruous yellow scarves, the symbol of the Sikh religion, around their necks, for they, along with others, had recently agreed to 'conversion.' These were the days of communal riots and the yellow scarf guaranteed security to the Muslim minority in East Punjab.

The Partition of the country had torn India into two and conversion had been made a condition by the Sikhs for those Muslims staying on in India, in retaliation to a similar declaration by Muslims in Pakistan for any Hindus or Sikhs there. The majority, no doubt, in our area were Muslims, and that too of the orthodox sect of Sunnis. But what could they do? They were in India and whoever did not convert to Sikhism was killed.

After the invitation for conversion a huge number of steel bangles, wooden crescent combs and yellow scarves were procured for an elaborate conversion ceremony. Just when the *parsad*[1], the sanctified sweet, was being prepared for initiating the Muslims to the Sikh religion, a phlegmatic voice said:

"What else do you advise us to do?"

"Feed them with pork," he said.

"Our own people have been made to eat beef on that side of the border", said another.

Everyone agreed to feed pork to the Muslims gathered for initiation. Four or five pigs were killed and cooked immediately. The ceremony had been carried out in a similar manner in the neighbouring villages.

The Muslims listened and watched with the resigned passivity and indifference of those who no longer cared whether they lived or died.

---

1 Parsad: The Punjabi colloquial form of prasad–a devotional offering made to a god, typically consisting of food that is later shared among devotees. It symbolises divine grace and kindness

"Our Gurus baptised with *parsad* only", my father whispered to Babaji, in mild protest.

"Keep your mouth shut, man. Nothing like silence," he said and drifted towards the pots of meat to examine the quality.

In a little while all the Muslims were initiated into the Sikh religion. Wearing the five symbols of Sikhism, they started swallowing the pieces of pork served to them.

"We have always been Hindus. Only that blasted Aurangzeb made us change", one of them said in a futile effort to seek justification for his acts. Babaji and few other village elders, sat a little separately from the rest, in their own superior elite group of Sandhus.

"The Maharaja of Patiala is a Sidhu", I heard him say. "Sidhu and Sandhu are equal. The only difference is that our *jagir* provides us only with opium while the maharaja's gives him all the luxury he could dream of." The talk did not interest me.

"'Noora and his people are not being baptised?" I asked my father. "Hush!" my father silenced me. "I have delivered all the five symbols to them and they are wearing them. Noora's father is a saintly person and respects us. I wouldn't want him to feel disgraced in public. May be he does not want to take part."

When my grandfather asked about the baptism of Badru and his family, my father managed to convince him that Badru had taken pork in his very presence. To allay any remaining doubts, father swore it solemnly and thus the whole of Badru's family was also counted among the baptised.

And where was the lie in it? That day when I had demanded the peacock feather from Rahmte she was wearing a yellow dupatta on her head and a steel bangle on her wrist. Her father Badru and her brother Noora too were wearing yellow scarves around their neck and steel bangles on their wrists. Both were performing the namaaz.

They would not have dared to pray the Muslim way had there been a witness. But then the only person present was myself and I was his pupil. They knew well that I would not tell anyone in the village that they were praying the Muslim way. How could I, who till the third standard had done my sums with the help of Rahmte?

It is still all so clear before my eyes, that day Rahmte carrying the sheaf of fodder, Badru and Noora praying. The long henna-dyed beard of the holy man touched the ground as he bowed in prayer. His loose *lucknawi* shirt was a little dirty. I stood at some distance watching them all, then I heard sudden shouts of "*Bole so Nihal, Sat Sri Akal.*" It was the Sikh cry and it sent us running for our lives in great terror. In the general panic Noora stumbled and fell on the ground. The running hoofs came to a stop and many a spear was jabbed viciously into his body. He lay there with his entrails hanging out. It was the last I saw of him.

I looked at the riders in yellow and blue and stood there dazed. They had already closed in on Badru. The saint pleaded with folded hands flourishing his yellow scarf and the steel bangle on his wrist to show he was a Sikh. A Nihang Sikh with fox-tail moustaches, playfully struck the arm which was raised to exhibit the bangle, and cut it clean from the elbow. When Badru raised his other hand in abject imploration, the tyrant struck that off too.

"Send this pig as well to Pakistan," someone shouted and ran towards me.

Sending one to Pakistan was a common phrase for killing a Muslim.

"He's a Sikh one, you fool", a voice checked him. It was the Nihang Sikh who had speared Noora.

From his saddle he lifted me up and put me in his lap.

I do not know what happened after that, for I lost consciousness.

When I came to my senses next day I was lying in bed in the verandah. My mother's eyes were red and swollen with crying.

"He's saved, don't you worry. It was only shock. He is just a child after all". Babaji was saying to my mother.

"It was almost the end of him", my mother said wiping her tears and rubbing my limbs.

"What a dreadful shock for you, my son! God protect you, God bless you," she said wiping my face with her dupatta.

"Bless and be blessed afterwards, first give offerings to the Martyrs who saved his life," said *Babaji* and everyone agreed to this proposal. They started making preparations for the Martyrs.

Choking, I told my mother about Noora's death and asked her in a trembling voice if she knew anything about Rahmte. She told me in tears that Jaina and Rahmte both had been abducted by the crusading rioters along with other Muslim girls of the village. Many were murdered, about fifty of them. Whoever was seen with a new yellow scarf and bright steel bangle was killed.

Meanwhile the whole of the village made ready to offer *parsad* to the Martyrs. Though it was a quiet evening, everyone was frightened. Baba Phuman Singh was absolutely stunned. He was almost out of his wits. Just a while ago he was informed that his life-long friend Ghanshyamdas had also been killed by mistake. He had been carrying a yellow scarf to one of his Muslim friends out in the fields, when he was surprised by the rioters who killed him, taking him to be a new convert. They did not wait to check who was who. They were busy people. They had to visit and plunder other villages too. For them the sight of a yellow scarf was enough to tell them of 'converts'.

While praying at the Martyrs' field, Babaji (my grandfather) was still thinking of Ghanshyamdas. Yes, true, he had to die some day. But this sudden and uncalled for death had signalled a new uncertainty to people, including Babaji. It meant that anyone who was carrying a yellow scarf, even if he was a Sikh or a Hindu, would not be spared. Where then was the guarantee of safety to converts? In fact those who had not accepted Sikhism were safer, for they were cautious, not caught so easily and hence not killed. Thus, absurdly, avowed Muslims were escaping while Sikhs were being slaughtered!

Even though he was singing aloud the praises of Guru Gobind's sons, the Five Beloved Ones, and the Forty Martyrs, his heart was crying over the calamitous riots. Towards the end, when he was reciting verses in honour of those who had shared their wealth, fought sinners, offered sacrifice for the faith suddenly his legs buckled beneath him. The mention of 'sacrifices for the faith' choked his throat. His *khunda* fell off to the ground. The rest of the prayer was completed by my father. Having finished the ceremony my father told me to go and offer *parsad* to the Martyrs. As I placed the *parsad* on their tombs, the crows from the peepul tree nearby came cawing and swooping and ate it up in no time. "'Let the Martyrs remain hungry," I said to myself.

As my father distributed *parsad* to everyone and was about to leave, Babaji came forward and held him there by his arm.

"Tell the boy to put some on the Pirs' tombs too", he said pointing towards the Pirs' graveyard. Looking in that direction I remembered Noora. The peepul in the field reminded me of Rahmte who had frowned at me under it. Had she done it in love or in hatred? I would never know now.

'What do you mean?' father asked Babaji, a little puzzled. "On the Pirs' tombs?"

"You remember the massacre", Babaji whispered to father, after taking him beyond the boundary of the field. Perhaps he dared not say it within the Martyrs' domain, afraid of their curse on his unbelief.

"Yes, I remember", father replied bitterly.

'Those who were initiated have been killed, haven't they?"

"So what?" whispered my father, still puzzled.

"Those who did not agree to initiation are saved, you know that."

"I don't understand", father said, frowning perplexedly.

"Well, if you don't, I can't help it", snapped Babaji, a little irritated by my father's denseness.

"Listen," he tried again, whispering very low to prevent the Martyrs overhearing. "Those who remained Muslims were saved, were they not? Well, who knows if tomorrow the Pirs don't turn out to be more powerful than our Martyrs?"

Suddenly enlightened, I ran and offered *parsad* at the Pirs' tombs. Father did not stop me.

Perhaps the insinuation in Babaji's remarks still escaped him?

Translation: Raj Gill

OF ONE COMMUNITY

Mohinder Singh Sarna

We were very happy – I and my mother, wife, son, daughter and three unmarried sisters – when we moved into the government flat on Satya Marg. This flat was smaller than the one we had lived in on Cornwallis Road; it had one bedroom and one bathroom less. That flat was in the C-II category, because there were too few of the C-I flats to which I was actually entitled. The Satya Marg flat was D-I, which was even lower than the C-II. But, as I said, we were all very happy to move, largely because of the surroundings in Chanakyapuri. This was where most of the foreign embassies were located, along the broad, clean avenues, resplendent with gulmohar trees. Chanakyapuri did not look like a part of Delhi; rather, it was as if someone had plucked out a piece of Washington, Paris or Frankfurt and placed it here.

I had asked for the move from Cornwallis Road to Satya Marg. I had been unwell, plagued by restlessness, through the year and a half that we had spent at Cornwallis Road. Though my condition was not new, it had assumed worrisome proportions during this period and the doctors had no clue. At long last one of the doctors suggested that a change of place might help, since he had found the Cornwallis Road area depressing. I saw sense in that suggestion. There was a ruined old tomb right across from our flat which was virtually the first thing I set my eyes on every morning. The sight of it at twilight filled me with dread. And when I went for an evening walk, I was confronted by the ruins of the Old Fort.

So even though the Satya Marg flat had only two bedrooms and two bathrooms we were happy to have put the ruins behind us. The new flat had a large study which could be turned into a bedroom. There was a covered balcony too that could be converted into another bedroom by enclosing it with windows. So we were not worried about the limited space. But a slight shadow had fallen on my mother's happiness when she learnt that our immediate neighbours were Muslims. Her mood had darkened visibly the moment she saw the nameplate on the door across the staircase.

"It doesn't matter, Mother," I said. "They will live in their own flat and we in ours. Only the staircase is shared and if we meet in passing we will greet each other. We are hardly likely to be close to them."

The riots that had accompanied the Partition of the country had left deep wounds in my mother's soul and planted a sharp antipathy towards Muslims in her heart. Her younger brother had been killed in Takht Pari and a cousin of mine in Basali. My mother's newlywed niece in Thoa Khalsa, had jumped into a well to save her honour while her husband had died fighting the mob of rioters. And we ourselves had barely managed to make it across the border, looted and bereft, after struggling in refugee camps and caravans, witnessing bloodshed and violence, and escaping death by a hair's breadth more than once.

She had convinced herself that Muslims were cruel, merciless and inhuman. I had often tried to remove this deep prejudice from her mind. I told her that the Hindus and Sikhs of East Punjab had behaved as viciously as the Muslims of West Punjab. Those who had committed these atrocities were neither Muslims, nor Hindus, nor Sikhs; barbarity has no religion. Their faith was merely barbarism, and they were the agents of Satan. My arguments had perhaps managed to take the edge off the hatred in my mother's heart, but it had not been completely wiped away. That was the reason that the presence of Muslim neighbours had cast a shadow over her joy at moving into the clean and pleasant environs of Chanakyapuri.

It was our first afternoon in the new house. We were all busy arranging our belongings. My wife was wiping the pictures and putting them up in the bedrooms. My sisters were setting up the pots, pans and crockery in the kitchen. In the drawing room, my mother was dusting the sofas and chairs, while I was unpacking the large wooden crate of books in the adjoining balcony. Just then there was a gentle knock on the front door. My mother unlatched the door and opened it. I peeped from the balcony to see who it was. A fair complexioned woman of about forty-five was standing at the door. She was dressed in a dark green sari and from the absence of a *bindi* on the forehead or *sindoor* in her parting, I surmised that she must be the wife of our neighbour, Shaukat Hussain.

"May I come in?" She asked in a soft, cultured tone.

"Come in." My mother opened the door fully.

I withdrew my head from the door and returned to dusting the books.

Since the sofas had not been dusted yet, Mother invited the lady to sit down on one of the dining chairs, which she had already cleaned, and sat down herself on another across from her.

"We live in the neighbouring flat, number 17. My husband is a Joint Secretary in the Ministry of Education. This flat of yours has been vacant for a couple of months. I can't tell you how happy we are that you have moved in."

I could hear her voice clearly as the dining table was very near the door behind which I was sitting.

Mother did not respond. She seemed taken aback at this unexpectedly early confrontation with our Muslim neighbours. Perhaps she was unconsciously comparing the visitor to the uneducated, *burqa* clad Muslim women she was used to encountering in Rawalpindi.

"You won't have eaten lunch because of your move. I'll send something over."

"No, no," Mother's refusal was unnecessarily emphatic and coloured with irritation.

'But why not? It can be ready in half an hour.'

"No, no," Mother repeated in the same tone. "There is no need for it. We had lunch before setting off." She was telling the truth: we had eaten lunch at Cornwallis Road.

"Then you will have dinner at our place tonight."

"No, no, how can that be? This cannot be."

The Begum seemed to have guessed the real reason for the refusal from my mother's flustered manner and the sharpness of tone. Her enthusiasm sagged a bit and she fell silent. I feared that Mother might say something that would ruin our relations with the neighbours on our very first day. I recalled that one day while travelling between Gujranwala and Rawalpindi she had drunk 'Muslim water' instead of 'Hindu water' at Lala Musa railway station. When a fellow traveller had pointed out that she had accepted water from a Muslim, she was overtaken by an urge to throw up. Her bout of nausea lasted for the rest of the journey. I sent my wife into the drawing room to save the situation.

The Begum, who was looking a bit low after her conversation with Mother, recovered her spirits on seeing Simran, my wife. She repeated the invitation for dinner.

"I was telling Mother that it would be nice if you had dinner with us tonight."

"We are very grateful," Simran replied in a very civil and patient tone, "but we really won't need to trouble you. The girls and I have set up the kitchen, and the gas is working too. If we happen to have any problem, we will come to you."

The refusal was the same, but the words and tone were different. Civility had been maintained, and both sides had saved face.

Just five minutes after the Begum had left, her soft knock sounded at the front door again. This time I opened the door. The Begum appeared a bit startled on seeing me but quickly gathered herself. She greeted me with a slight nod of her head, unable to raise her hand in greeting as she was holding two plates, one with bananas and melon slices and the other heaped with dry fruits.

"Come, please come in."

Simran too had come into the drawing room on hearing the door open.

"Oh, there was no need for all this," she said. 'Why did you take so much trouble?'

"No trouble at all," the Begum said. "It's a pleasure. Please don't refuse this time."

Simran raised no objection and put both plates on the dining table. Happiness that we had accepted the fruits she had brought, and disappointment that we had refused the food cooked in her house, began to play a strange game of hide-and-seek on the Begum's face.

Just then Mother came into the room to see who had come now.

"My husband also wanted to come and meet you," the Begum, said, "but he is not too well today. He didn't even go to his office."

"What's the matter?" I asked.

"He begins to feel very restless all of a sudden. His legs go weak and his hands start to tremble. He gets such strong attacks of this restlessness and discomfort that it seems his life is in danger."

Mother, Simran and I exchanged looks. These were the symptoms of my own condition, which had troubled me for so many years.

"What do the doctors say?" Simran asked.

"The doctors all believe that there is nothing wrong with him. His heart, his blood pressure, his blood sugar are all fine. They say that all these years he has nurtured a delusion that he is ill."

Again we exchanged glances. The doctors had said exactly the same to me all these years.

"This morning Dr. Bose came and said that now there was only one thing left to do. We have to consult a good neurologist."

"And?" I asked.

"We've called Dr. Sukhdev Singh, the top neurologist at Willingdon Hospital. He's coming at five today. Let's see what he says."

At about a quarter to six in the evening, I glanced out of the drawing room window and saw a doctor carrying a bag getting into a car.

"Simran," I called out to my wife. "It seems that the neurologist has seen Shaukat Hussain Sahib. We should go to their house and ask after him."

"I will also come with you," Mother said. She was clearly keen to see what opinion the neurologist had given on the condition that our neighbour and I shared.

Shaukat Hussain Sahib was lying in bed. When he saw us, he propped himself up on a pillow. On seeing us in her home, the Begum seemed to forget all about her husband's illness.

"Please sit here. Be comfortable. Mother, you please sit here," she fussed over us.

"What did the neurologist say?" asked Simran.

"Well, he started by checking the heart and blood pressure," the Begum related. "Then he wanted to know my husband's entire history, right from childhood. Who used to scold you in childhood? Did anybody hit you? Did any servant frighten you when you were alone at home? Was your grandfather a very short-tempered man? Was the atmosphere at home happy or terrifying? Was there any teacher who you feared? Did you have any accident or tragedy in your childhood or youth? When my husband replied in the negative to all these questions, the doctor was lost in thought. Then it was as if a sudden light turned on in his mind and he asked, "Where were you during Partition?"

The Begum fell silent suddenly. As if some wild animal had jumped at her from the dark past. We waited as she gathered herself. When she spoke, there was a quiver in her voice.

"He told the doctor that he was then in Moradabad. The mob of rioters burnt down his ancestral haveli. They killed his father and two uncles, and raped his sister-in-law and two unmarried sisters."

Everyone knew that Simran was foolish. Her eyes immediately filled with a veritable storm of tears at any sad story. And that's exactly what happened. The tears were flowing freely down her cheeks. Then I saw that tears had welled up in Mother's eyes too.

"And then?" I asked, my voice choked with emotion.

"Then it seemed the doctor had got a grip on the problem. He wanted to know every detail of those evil days and terrible nights.

His opinion was that the horror and fear of the Partition riots had settled deep into my husband's subconscious mind and it was that which caused these bouts of restlessness and despair. He said that it was not a delusional belief but a serious psychological condition which needed to be treated properly. And that it could be cured."

I looked at Simran, she looked at me and Mother looked at both of us. Our looks said that in one fell swoop, my own condition had been diagnosed.

"I am convinced of the neurologist's advice," the Begum continued. "It was only after Partition that my husband began to suffer these attacks. In the months of August-September, the time when these riots took place, he always suffers from them."

Wiping the tears from her face with her dupatta, Simran said, "You will be surprised to learn that my husband suffers from the same problem. All of a sudden he loses heart. 'I'm dying,' he says. 'Call the doctor, do something.' All these years, no doctor has been able to understand his problem."

Holding back the rush of tears, Mother added: "We also saw a lot of bloodshed during the Partition riots. We suffered big blows, terrible losses. It appears our two families have the same illness."

"We have the same illness," I spoke in my mother's support, "because we belong to one community."

Seeing the quizzical looks in the eyes of Simran and my mother, I continued. "I am right. There are only two communities in this world: the cruel and the meek. Our two families belong to the community of the meek."

I saw that Shaukat Hussain was nodding in agreement.

"Bhabi-jaan,'" I said involuntarily, and then I hesitated. "Can I take the liberty of calling you Bhabi-jaan?"

"Of course, Bhai-sahib. Why not?"

"Bhabi-jaan, this is a happy moment. A wise neurologist has diagnosed the illness in both our families. Diagnosis is half the cure. The rest is just a matter of time. And then once we're totally cured, Shaukat Hussain Sahib and I will go for long walks from Satya Marg to Shanti Path. So like I said, it's a happy moment. Give us something sweet."

"Why not, Bhai-sahib," the Begum replied. "I'll get some fruit, and some dry fruit too."

"Forget those," I said. "If you're going to give us something sweet, then do it properly."

"But how?" The Begum asked, a trifle helplessly.

"Maybe some *halwa* with raisins or some *kheer* with coconut and almonds, or a nice dish of *sevian*."

The Begum looked at Simran and then at Mother. The open smiles on both their faces were supporting my request.

"We understand your problem, Bhabi jaan", I said. "Making any of these dishes takes time. We're in no hurry. We're as comfortable as we would be in our own home. We'll content ourselves with tea and biscuits until the real sweet dish is ready."

The Begum jumped up with joy and rushed happily towards the kitchen, calling out, "I'll be back in an instant," as she went.

Translation: Navtej Sarna

FATTU THE BARD

Gurbachan Singh Bhullar

One day when Fattu the bard, his wife, Kariman, his two sons, Yusuf and Hamida suddenly returned to the village from Pakistan, it became the sole topic of conversation in the entire village. The people went to meet Fattu and his family and Fattu visited every household in the village. He seemed to have an age-old, unquenchable thirst that he was trying to slake at every house. He would come out of one house and enter the next, saying, "Greetings, Chachi.... Sat Sri Akal, Brother Sohan Singh.... Bibi Dyal Kaur, is this Guddi? The blessed child has grown into a young woman behind my back."

He sat for ages with the elders of the village and chatted about joys and sorrows, home and the world, friends and relatives. A wave of affection rose in his breast when he met people and he would be overwhelmed. He wandered about in the streets of the village for many days. Kariman visited the older women of the village and talked about common concerns.

Fattu was the ancestral bard of Sukhwant's village. Before Pakistan was carved out, Sukhwant and Fattu's son, Yusuf, had been classmates in middle school. Although Yusuf belonged to a low-caste family, there was a deep bond of friendship between the two. Sukhwant would accompany him home several times. The day Yusuf had his *sunnat* (circumcision) ceremony, he had eaten jaggery to his heart's content in his house. Yusuf called Fattu 'Chacha', aping his cousins. Fattu was, in any case, younger than Sukhwant's father was; so he also called him Chacha.

Then came 1947. From near and far, vague rumours began to reach us. Initially, people found it difficult to believe them. How could it be? But ultimately, violence erupted in this area too. Fattu's middle son, Basheera, had gone to his maternal grandparents' home and the news was that all the Muslims in that place had been killed. God's will had similarly prevailed in the village where Fattu's daughter, Niyamat, had been married. But who had the time to inquire after anybody else?

Rumours were rife that within the next few days, the neighbouring marauders would raid this village. Even here, the village rogues had begun to sharpen their hatchets. Some influential elders of the village held a conference and helped all the Muslims of the village to cross the border near Ferozepur within the hour.

Later it was known that a hatchet had embedded itself deep into Basheera's head and had run till the nose, and that Niyamat's family members had been killed and she had been abducted by some rogues.

Then, letters from Fattu and many other Muslims began to be received in the village. Whatever he had managed to muster and carry with him as he had fled from home, had been snatched soon after crossing the border, and he had stepped on the land of the Mohammedans, empty-handed. Seva Singh, Sukhwant's father, received several letters from Fattu. Apart from the usual courtesies, one question was repeatedly raised—about the whereabouts of Basheera and Niyamat.

Whenever Fattu thought of his grown up daughter and youthful son left behind, he burst into lamentations. This obsession brimmed over from his letters. He repeatedly begged the Pakistani police that rescued Muslims from Hindustan, to take him along with them so that he could search for his own flesh and blood. But each time he was told to get the address of his son and daughter before petitioning to be taken along. He begged Seva Singh to trace the whereabouts of his children....

But Seva Singh could not muster the courage to reveal the truth. He wrote back to say that some Muslims had been killed in those two villages, and the rest had escaped. There was no news about Basheera and the girl.

And then even the letters stopped.

The storm blew over; people began to repent. People like Fattu the bard, were often remembered. Sukhwant was unable to forget his companion, Yusuf. Years passed and the events prior to '47 and the people prior to '47 became dim memories for the people.

Sukhwant's steps slowed down whenever he passed by Fattu's house. Their house had not been allotted to anyone. All the Muslims of this village had been landless menials. The land of the Muslim landlords had been allotted to the refugees from Pakistan, but neither did any 'Pakistani' come to such a village, nor did the houses of the Muslims find new residents. Either the neighbouring houses swallowed them up or they lay abandoned, deteriorating into ruins with people dumping their garbage there. Gradually the bricks and mortar from Fattu's house disappeared, and now there was a bare space there, where, more often than not, animals sat down to chew the cud.

When Fattu the bard, his wife, Kariman, his sons, Yusuf and Hamida returned to the village, at first, they felt despondent to see the bare ground where their home had once stood. But the people consoled them. If they had returned now to stay, there was nothing to worry about. All of them would support him and his family.

A few bricks here, some gravel there, some beams of wood, some chains, and Fattu had erected two small rooms with a roof and an outer wall. For several days, he wandered from door to door, invoking the grace of God to beg for the requisite things.

Once he was through with the roofing of his rooms, Fattu took charge of his place in life like an employee who has been transferred. Whenever there was a wedding or a death in the village, he would go and squat in the courtyard in God's name. He would run whatever errands he was asked to. He would run to call whoever it was who had to be called. His younger son, Hamida, who had learnt the trade of a barber in Pakistan, found work with a city barber. His elder son, Yusuf, would carry wedding presents for people and news of deaths to relatives in other villages.

The winter crop was ready for harvest. By now, Fattu had saved some money of his own; and the rest he collected from each household and bought a pair of ponies. He requested work from the harvesters and through carrying of these loads made enough money to lead a comfortable life.

Although Fattu was as content as only a man who has returned after serving a sentence of exile can be, the memory of Basheera and Niyamat had become a cancerous tumour in his bosom. He would often sit against the wall of the courtyard with his eyes closed, smoking a hukkah. He would feel as if Basheera and Niyamat were playing about the courtyard, or running in the street. As if Basheera was carrying his satchel to school, and Niyamat was helping Kariman with the household chores, and then he would remember the catastrophic days....

He would be unable to think further. The pipe of the hukkah would slip from his mouth and tears would run down his cheeks into his beard in two thin rivulets. He would brace himself and wipe his tears with the tail of his kurta and get a grip on himself. He would try to engross himself completely in his work and forget everything else.

Once, on his way to the grain market, Sukhwant bumped into Fattu, and the latter asked him the date of Sukhwant's wedding. After being told that it was seven days away, he said, "All right, Prabha. By then I would be through with the digging of the pond of the *bohad* trees. It seems as if they have forgotten how to dig a tank while I was away! Once it rains, buffaloes will sit comfortably in the pit. Moreover, the roots of the peepal and *bohad* trees are showing through as the soil on the edges of the tank has eroded."

Before Pakistan was made, Fattu bestirred himself every year and the pond by the *bohad*s would be dug out. His drum echoed, resonated, and the shovels dug deeper and deeper. Platforms were embanked under the surrounding *bohad* trees. In these years, the soil of the tank had been dug out, but it might as well have not been, for all the good it did.

Sukhwant said, "Chacha, even if they dig the tank by themselves, it won't help. Only if you take it on, will it work."

And Fattu agreed to take on the job. The next day, people went to it with shovels. Fattu would encourage the diggers with his drum, and also wander around the village to inspire other people to leave home and contribute to the digging, and to ask the older women to provide sweetened tea and milk.

People worked as if possessed by demons, and, within three days, finished digging the entire tank.

And Fattu put down his drum.

Since the previous day, Fattu had been dancing about like a bobbin at the wedding in Sukhwant's *taya*'s house. Managing accounts and sundries was Sukhwant's responsibility. Cots and beddings had been collected from the neighbours the day before. Fattu, along with two servants, had visited seven-eight houses at a time, returned and pasted slips on the cots with the names of the owners with Sukhwant's help. Today, the invitations had to be sent out and he had prepared a list of the houses in a notebook.

Fattu asked Sukhwant to list fifteen to twenty families along one side of a page. Once that was done, he wrote the corresponding addresses of their houses on the other side and left for his rounds. Sukhwant counted eighteen houses on one side alone. He drew a mental map of all the houses. Then according to his map, he enumerated the eighteen houses—the houses of all four corporals, the three houses of the sarpanch, three houses of the barefoot ones, both the houses of the birdcatchers, Surjan's, Godha's, Makhan Singh's, Darbara Singh's, Dayal Singh's, Surat's. And he set off at a brisk pace, adjusting his shoulder-cloth on his left shoulder and picking up his stick placed against the neem tree.

Sukhwant sat down on the stump of the tree under the neem, thinking about Fattu and the clan of bards and their memory.

Before Pakistan was born, bards would be present on every occasion – happy or sad – wedding or funeral. Once things had been explained and the houses pointed out to them, they wouldn't miss even a single one. They would neither evade work, nor grow weary of it.

Several days ago, Sukhwant had gone to the gurudwara to read the paper, and heard Bhaiji telling Fattu, "Mardana has said that life was very difficult without you. To collect all the Keerat Singhs of our village is no easy task. When you were away, we used to ask the watchman, and he would make excuses, and say, 'One *kirtaniya* Singh is at one end of the village, another at the other end, the third at yet another edge; my knees refuse to support me.'"

And Fattu, as he did before '47, would wake up as the cock rooster crowed if someone had organised a kirtan of *Asan di vaar*. He would round up every *kirtaniya* and then guide the blind musician, Nand Singh, by the arm to escort him to the house where the kirtan was to be held.

When Fattu was returning from the eighteenth house, he saw Har Kaur who was visiting her parental house, seated in the doorway of her brother, Santa barber's house. The rest of the family was indoors. Inquiring after her wellbeing, Fattu squatted beside her cot. They sat rummaging through the ashes of the past that had once been a raging fire, and was almost extinct now with the assaults of time and the passage of years. Fattu remarked as he got up to leave, rolling up his sleeves, "We left everything there for the second time, but I still wear the silver amulet that you brought from the fair of Gurusar on my arm!"

There was nothing more to be said between them, and he hurried towards Sukhwant's house with long strides.

After greeting him with an "Allah Khair" Fattu stood before Sukhwant, "Here, Prabha, I've been to all the eighteen houses. Open your notebook and check; I might have gone to the wrong house." And he began to count all the houses, "All the four houses of the corporals, the three houses of the sarpanch, the three houses of the barefoot ones, both of the birdcatchers, Surjan's...."

"That's fine, Chacha. It is just not possible that you can invite the wrong household!" Sukhwant said, "There's some tea, have some before you start on the other side. Sit here."

Fattu sat down on the ground before him. Sukhwant wanted to chat with Fattu. Ever since Fattu had returned from Pakistan and Sukhwant had talked to Yusuf a couple of times, this question had been bothering him. Yusuf had been unable to answer this question. The entire family did whatever Fattu said and followed his directions.

Yusuf had told him how, after wandering about a bit in Pakistan, they had found a place just large enough to shelter them and which still had some odds and ends lying about. With hard labour, they had begun to get two square meals a day. Then why did Fattu return here after so many years?

During the course of the conversation, he did ask the question, "Chacha, when you were managing a good living there, what made you come back here?"

"Prabha, one's people are one's own people," he looked deep into his eyes.

"Chacha, don't feel hurt thinking of past events, but how can the people who have hacked your Basheera and abducted your Niyamat, be your own people?" Sukhwant became emotional thinking of what had befallen Fattu.

Fattu turned sorrowful and began to weep. He sat down crossing his legs, as if he could no longer sit on his haunches. He sat silently for a few minutes, idly drawing pictures in the sand, as if he was swallowing something and trying to locate the lineaments of Basheera and Niyamat in the sand. Then, he took a grip on himself, and wiped the tears with the corner of his towel, "That, Prabha, was a storm... a black, thunderous storm. Everybody had lost his senses. Who is to blame? It was a catastrophe sent down by Allah. The storm came and died down; now what is the use of remembering it?"

Dissatisfied by this answer Sukhwant asked, "No, Chacha, whether you agree or not, you must have suffered in Pakistan. We've heard that the condition of the people there is even worse than that of the people here?"

"It's hardly any different from here, Prabha. One could get by," he said, combing the soil he had dug out with a blade of grass.

"Then...why? Where was the need? Once you had already been forced to abandon a prosperous household because of the birth of Pakistan. Now again you abandon the Pakistan that you had yourself created?"

Fattu looked down and was silent. Sukhwant kept staring at him, but didn't say anything. Then Fattu looked straight at him with his piercing, blazing eyes and said, "Prabha, it was hardly my house and land. We were not allowed to stay in Hindustan, and no one considered us Pakistanis. We were '*muhajirs*', 'refugees', 'poor souls'!"

And then he scooped up a fistful of sand and touched it to his forehead with his eyes closed, "Prabha, this is what pulled me back. This is what was missing there!"

Translation: Hina Nandrajog

WITHOUT A HOMELAND

Prem Parkash

I had secured the job of an editor of a weekly called *Industrialist*, run by one of the big shots in a large city. However I had not found any accommodation as yet. The biggest disadvantage of staying in the office was that the proprietor always kept an eye on my movements: what I ate, when I slept or woke up....

After several fruitless attempts I learnt about a house that was situated on the outskirts of the city, on the road leading to a village. Soon I discovered that the acquaintance who had informed me about it had fooled me. An elderly professor who, according to my source, was half-mad, was living in that particular four-room old-fashioned bungalow

When I reached the house I saw a man planting a sapling just inside the gate. Startled by my greeting he stood up, raising his eyebrows frowningly to ask 'what is it?' as he dusted the soil off his hands. I was convinced I had reached the right place and met the right man. When I enquired about the vacant room he refused flatly, and walked off to wash his hands at the water pump. My need was urgent, so I darted forward to work the pump for him. He leapt and placed his soiled hand next to mine, glaring. I stepped back. He pulled out the clean edge of his shirt from his khaki trousers and wiped his hands. This was the first cue that he wasn't 'all there'. But I was so desperate that even a butcher's abode would have been acceptable to me.

His brows creased and furrows formed on his forehead. Lost in thought, he started walking towards me as if I was not there at all and he had been all alone. I was reminded of a Persian saying about eccentric people being clever enough when their own interests are involved. I followed him inside. There were two chairs and a table on the verandah. He halted suddenly as if he had perceived a ghost behind him. I scrutinised the house. Constructed in the Islamic style, the house consisted of only four rooms. Next to the verandah at the back was a huge garden with flowering shrubs and vegetables. On the facade of the house was engraved 'Trust God's Will'.

All this while, I continued to express my desperation and he turned his face towards me, but spoke as if he were addressing a tree or a table, "There's one condition. I shouldn't ever feel your presence here."

I agreed immediately. At that time even if he had asked me to abandon my soul and throw only my body in the house, I would have jumped at the offer.

It was an airy room, neither too warm nor too cold. I would sleep indoors. When I'd wake up in the morning, Professor Sahib would either be cleaning the hen-coops or tending to his chickens, or he'd be gardening. I seldom stayed at home and whenever I did, I would keep myself busy preparing my meal or reading a book in bed.

About twenty days passed like this. He seemed to have no objections to my stay. Whenever he passed by my room he would steal a look inside from the corner of his eyes. At times when his pet lamb or his cat-sized dog, Jackie, would sneak into my room he would follow them inside and carry them away. With a quick look at my sparse belongings he would beat a hasty retreat. Initially the fact that he kept so many pets irritated me, but by and by I too started keeping aside some crumbs for Jackie and waited for him.

The Professor's repeated saunterings into my room made me realise that he was trying to express his acceptance of my presence. Once, I did not go to office. There wasn't much work and I was running a mild fever. The Professor hovered around my room the whole day and when that evening, his sole friend, a retired army doctor, did not arrive, he turned up in my room. Addressing the walls he issued an invitation, "Come, have a cup of tea." I had been yearning for tea but had lacked the energy to make it for myself. I rose and sat in one of the chairs in the verandah to enjoy the cup of tea. We had nothing to converse about. For the sake of making small talk, we spoke about Doctor Sahib, who, for some reason, had not put in an appearance that day.

After that we would have an occasional cup of tea together. During this period I learnt that the Professor had no close relatives. There was only a distant cousin who would visit him once in a while. The Professor had been teaching in a Lahore college and his wife and children had got left behind there. Here, he owned a small piece of land that took care of his needs. Also, some person sent him a little money. Doctor Sahib who visited him regularly was his friend from Lahore.

It was a major ordeal to think of topics to discuss during tea time. If at all there was any conversation between us, it pertained to his numerous pets. Most of the time he remained silent but sometimes he talked passionately about the habits of his pets, and would rattle off a lot of information that did have the charm of novelty initially, but soon became boring.

On another occasion, Doctor Sahib again did not turn up. Both of us sat in the verandah sipping tea. These were the days when Pakistan had attacked the Rann of Kutch. The newspapers were dishing out hot news about the war in bold headlines. Committees had been set up for collection of funds for the defence forces. I, too, was preparing inspiring material for a special issue of the magazine, calculated to rouse patriotic fervour in the hearts of the industrialists and the industrial labour and motivate them to join the war preparations.

I mentioned this to Professor Sahib, hoping to inspire him to write some article or contribute towards the funds. In the process, I thought I could publish his photograph and bring him some recognition. I hoped to kill two birds with one stone: gratify his ego as well as serve the nation. I felt pleased with myself, convinced that he would not only agree to my proposal but also look at me approvingly. In fact he might even waive off my rent.

To my surprise, he first seemed a little irritated at my proposal, and then burst out laughing. "The truth is I don't possess an iota of patriotism. It might have existed once but now it cannot be invoked by any amount of prodding."

Such words from a fairly educated man seemed inappropriate. Though I was loathe to get into an argument with him, yet I could not help bursting out, "Professor Sahib, can we sit quietly if a foreign power attacks us and enslaves the land that nurtures us?"

He did not answer my question and continued smoking. I repeated, "This is a moment of truth for the nation. Today to safeguard every bit of our land, every child of the nation must...." His laughter cut me short, though he said nothing. I watched him, angry and perplexed. I was also a little embarrassed at the choice of my own words; it sounded too much like the headline of a newspaper or a statement from the Prime Minister.

Abruptly he bent forward, and flicking the ash from the cigarette into the ashtray, asked me, "Which country, which culture, what nation are you talking of?" What could I say in answer? After a pause he continued, "I have no country. I was born in Lahore and educated in England. Though I spent many years there my country was always Hindustan. In 1944, I returned to India. In 1947, I realised that my country was somewhere on the other side of Wagah. Now there's a clamouring for Khalistan, and I do not know where my nation will be tomorrow."

He continued passionately. "A major part of a culture is its religion. People of so many religions live here but for a Muslim – apart from Mecca-Medina – Pakistan and other Muslim countries are *his* nation. Sikhs do not consider anything beyond Punjab as *their* nation! Someone who fights for every piece of land! The people living in the villages near Kutch which is now in Pakistan, were Indians till yesterday and ready to lay down their lives for every bit of *this* land; today they are Pakistanis and ready to die for *that* land."

He paused and lit a new cigarette. It struck me that he must be a communist who disagrees with the barriers and boundaries of nations and envisions the whole world as a global family. Only a fool would try to convince such a person. I held my peace. He resumed, "Nation! People don't have any concept of a nation or nationhood.

Nor will it ever be developed. Nor is that necessarily a bad thing when the greater needs of the people are food and education."

My guess was right. When a person gives priority to food, he is a communist. Though I was a little upset, I spoke calmly, "The matter of the country is straightforward—just like this house of yours where you live. Here you have your flowers and plants, your animals. You love even these walls. If someone attacks this house of yours, injures you and throws you out, how would you feel? Will you not guard your house?"

He was further ruffled by this argument. He puffed at the cigarette and snarled, "When my parents died in an accident in England I came to Lahore, thinking that a person can live with dignity only in his own nation. When my wife and children were snatched from me and I was thrown out of my house, what could I do...? Here the people you threw out of their homes, their nation, what harm did they ever do you? Living here, my condition is even worse than that of the Jews, who at least have a nation now. I have no nation!"

These pointless arguments annoyed me. I could not control myself. "You may or may not accept it, but as far as I am concerned, this is my country. Those who have no consideration for it have no right to live here."

My words left him dumbstruck. I was quite pleased with myself; even though there was no logic in my argument, it had the force enough to silence him.

Professor Sahib's face smouldered. He glared at me. His face blazed. The cigarette began to shake in his fingers. Then suddenly he exploded, "*Your country*! Is it *your* country? You! You who have to go around wagging your tail like a wretched dog to rent a room! Whose three generations have lived in a rented house! One who has to run from pillar to post to earn his bread and butter! You consider yourself an editor! Playing with the sentiments of people!" He lambasted me and jumping out of the chair rushed indoors, muttering to himself, "Shame on me! Shame that I am a citizen of this contemptible nation! When did I ever think I would live in this country of fools and cheats! Oh! For heavens' sake, give me freedom; leave me alone."

Once inside, he seemed to calm down. I sat outside repenting my folly in having revealed so much of my family background to him. How undignified I had rendered myself in his eyes! Poor, worthless, homeless! How many taunts I had to bear! Why did I ever start this discussion! For all I knew, he might even throw me out tomorrow itself!

For a long time I sat immersed in my thoughts. Finally I decided to beg forgiveness and bring him around. When I went inside I found him sprawled on his bed with his shoes still on. His face was pale as that of a woman who has just miscarried. As I looked at him a wave of sorrow surged inside me. I felt that not only he but I too had no homeland.

Dragging my leaden feet, I returned to my room like one who has just returned from bearing the bier of a dear one on his shoulders to the crematorium and performing the last rites. But I felt very restless. I opened the gate and went out. It had turned dark. Trudging on the footpath of the village I reached the bridge over the stream where nothing but the gurgle of water could be heard.

Translation: Madhuri Chawla

YOU WILL ALWAYS BE MY WORLD

Gurbaksh Singh Preetlari

A jungle of tall rosewood trees flanked the wide sinuous canal. In the summer months, this jungle was a haven for birds, travellers and students studying for their examinations. Outside, the sunlight would scorch, the furnace would burn; inside, the fresh gusts of breeze, cooled as they rustled through the branches over the grassy green carpet, enticed one to forget the worries of the weather and the exams. Birds hopped and chirped musical notes in this green solitude, and amorous peacocks wooed their mates in all their splendour.

A tall, slim, well-built youth stepped off the pavement and hurried into the jungle. He sat down on a patch of thick, smooth grass. His turban proclaimed him to be Sikh, but when, after glancing all around, he took it off and placed it by his side, one could see that he did not have the long hair traditional to Sikhs. His chin was, as yet, innocent of any beard, but downy hair covered his upper lip. He had fine features and thoughtful, meditative eyes. Even at such a tender age, his wheat-complexioned face reflected a strange determination.

Just then an elderly gentleman came towards him from the direction of their village. He smiled and sat down beside him. He sported an uncut beard and a turban that had not been creased properly. His features were coarse and complexion dark. In short his expression suggested that his inner being was not in harmony with his outer self.

"Why, Kurban, been waiting long? Swarna got me talking at the well – about you – but he wouldn't finish."

"No, I also got delayed at home. Ma asked me to do something – I can't refuse her – but what did Swarna have to say about me?"

"Only wondered if you will stay or not—in six months it will be time for the condition of your guardian to be fulfilled."

"And what did you say?"

"I'm no longer in the habit of speaking the truth.... I said, 'Where will he go, he'll stay with us, he'll be a Sikh like us....' But tell me honestly, what *do* you intend to do?"

"The same as I have always told you...I'll definitely not become a Sikh—I cannot live with my mother's murderers."

"But are you absolutely certain that these wicked men will permit you to go? Swarna has already declared, 'Only let him mention going and we'll tear him apart!'"

"One can't expect anything better from them, but I trust my Sardar. He said that he would ensure that my independent decision prevails. He has some influential officer friends and said to me, 'If you stay, I'll be happy; if you wish to go, to honour your decision would be my duty.' You know the kind of person he is!"

"He's an angel, not a man – that's why everyone has sent me to you – you must go and meet all our relatives there. Give them our messages. Write down all their addresses and go from door to door. Tell them how we yearn to meet them. Tell them how we think and talk about them all day and through the night!"

They embraced and stood up. One walked towards the village and the other ascended the path along the canal.

Both were Muslims. Kurban lived in a Sikh household. The other had been converted to Sikhism, along with many other Muslims, in the holocaust of 1947. Those who had refused to convert to Sikhism in this village had either been hacked to death or drowned in the canal. Kurban had been five years old then. His mother, along with five other women with children had been herded to a spot on the bank of the canal. Some of them had infants in their arms. The savages had come with *kirpans*. Every child had been hacked twice and hurled into the canal. Kurban's mother had attempted to hug him one last time when a sword had swooped down and killed her in front of his eyes. At that very moment, the Sardar in whose house Kurban had found a home, had come to stand between him and the killer.

"You've done whatever you had to; now don't try to sharpen your blade on the body of this child.... Beware, Kahlia, don't raise your sword; it'll have to go through me.... Go ahead if you really want to!"

Kahle's raised arm fell before the Sardar's hoary beard, his magnetism, his whole bearing and his authoritative tone.

Kurban had been raised in the Sardar's house. The Sardar's only daughter had been about two years old at that time and was the only ray of sunshine in his dreary childhood. Now she was growing up. She was not yet fifteen but people called her the Sardar's Pathani daughter. She was ripening into a real beauty. Since she was always called Sohni, the beautiful one, her mother had not given her a formal name. "Once she grows up, we'll baptise her and christen her Sohan Kaur," Ma would say.

Kurban had also grown into a handsome youth. The Sardar and the Sardarni had brought him up like a son, but several leaders of the village had not been able to bear this. When he had turned ten, they had come in a group to the Sardar. "A shorn Kurban doesn't adorn an Adi Sikh household. People talk. This Sakranti convert him to Sikhism."

The Sardar, an engineer, had retired from an important position with a handsome pension. He was famed for following his own inclination. Fair-mindedness was important to him. "You are welcome to my house," the Sardar had said, "but with due respect, I cannot forget the time when I was unable to save his mother from your wrath. Now that the frenzy and tempest have abated, I will not permit any more injustice done to him!"

"What injustice? We are only asking you to improve his after-life. And look here, Sardarji, you keep harping on our savagery and forget what befell Bishan Singh. After ten members of his family were killed before his eyes, God knows how he managed to reach here; he tells how they axed trainloads and how they filled wells with the corpses of women!"

"What Bishan Singh narrates is also the limit of barbarity, but you have taken an eye for an eye. Life has blessed me with a lot of happiness and I am doing my duty in order to express my gratitude to the Almighty. The boy is ten years old today. To change his religion at this point of time is coercion. Let him turn eighteen, treat him well, he will study and play with Sikh boys only – he'll become a Sikh voluntarily – even now, does he behave like a Mussalman?"

Eight years had passed. Kurban was nearly eighteen. Lying in wait for his decision at the approaching Sakrant, there were as many opinions as tongues in the village. People even feared a disturbance.

The Sardar was a veritable rock. If it came to a confrontation, then he was a one-man army. He had conceded defeat only once in his life—during the holocaust of 1947. He had paced about like a caged tiger. His grieving soul had been throttled impotent behind the bars of the cage.

But now he had got a hold on himself. Many young men of the village respected him for his sense of justice and he was on good terms with the elders outside. He would be extremely happy if Kurban elected to stay. But if he wished to leave, then the Sardar's happiness would lie in ensuring that Kurban got justice even if he had to lay his own life on the line.

Although Kurban had discussed his decision to leave with his close friends, he was also aware of two major obstacles in his path. One was the thought of the travails that his Sardar would have to undertake in sending him to Pakistan.

Four days ago, the Sardar had summoned Kurban to ask about his decision. As the moment of decision had come closer, sadness had prevailed over Kurban. He had even lost his appetite.

"I'll do whatever you want, Bapuji," he had answered after a long silence when the Sardar had posed the query.

"No, my son, this will be your soul's decision—I have no right to impose my desire. Your decision will be my duty."

"But if my decision disturbs the peace – if someone causes hardship to my mother and sister – I will prefer death to such a decision."

"Don't worry about any such thing. I have examined all the pros and cons of your decision and I have, as a matter of precaution, made all arrangements and tied up every loose end. The day you announce your final decision, I'll send you to the city with a letter to a friend. He will make the rest of the arrangements with the High Commissioner of Pakistan. And he'll buy all the necessities for you

– don't take anything from here – and don't you worry about your mother and sister; no one dare lift a finger at them while I'm alive."

"Then Bapuji, I would like to go to Pakistan," Kurban had said, raising his eyes.

"I promise you'll go, Kurban," and the Sardar had hugged him.

But this was not the only major obstacle in his path. It was the Sardar's daughter, whom he had played with as a child and whom he ferried to school and back on the seat of his bicycle.

The melody of the birds on the fragrant, flowering branches of the *kikar* trees on the left side of the canal, the frothy dance of the frisky waves on the right, a Kashmiri twig basket with Sohni's books in the front, and the soft touch of Sohni's hands, sitting on the seat at the back, prattling sweetly throughout the way—these were the only few moments when Kurban would forget the terrifying memories of his childhood.

There was a farewell tea party in Sohni's school for the final year students. While bringing her back from school, Kurban was unusually quiet.

"Veer, why aren't you speaking properly today?" Sohni upbraided him.

"Because I will not have the pleasure of giving Sohni a ride again."

"Why not? Take me every evening; Bapuji won't say anything."

"He won't say anything—but...but..."

"But what?' Sohni demanded, prodding his back.

"No, Sohni, nothing; you'll soon go to a college in a big city...and I..." Sohni felt that his voice had become suddenly leaden.

"And you, I know, will never leave Maji, Bapuji and me to go anywhere. I'll erase all your bitter memories; do you hear me, my Veer?" And she stretched her arms wider to hug his waist.

By the time they reached home and dismounted from the bicycle, Kurban was wiping his eyes. Sohni could not, even in her wildest dreams, imagine that Kurban had decided to leave their house. He had often told Sohni, "You'll get married, Sohni. God knows where you'll go off to; no one will even let me look at you." Then Sohni would hold out her hand and say, "If you don't want me to marry, then I won't; at least, no one is going to ask us to leave *this* house."

"But Sohni, this can't be! A Jat's daughter will definitely get married…and that, too, to some big Sardar. Once you leave this village – this village of my mother's killers – will close upon me. No, Sohni, I am determined to go to Pakistan," Kurban blurted out.

Sohni reared up like a lioness as if her eyes had been opened to the bitter reality for the first time. Kurban also stood up and looked at Sohni. Her appearance was even more entrancing than ever before: her braided hair swung like black coils on each shoulder. A well-formed chin with a small indentation, luscious lips naturally puckered, through which her teeth gleamed like a string of pearls. A blush of tempestuous youth on her cheeks, long sharp nose, delicate nostrils, thin but flared due to anxiety, soul-searching eyes that could sear to the very heart under thick, silken eyebrows and a forehead that shone like the moon on a dark night under shining black hair. She wore a white shirt, embroidered at the collar with black thread, hinting at burgeoning breasts. There was a string with red beads around a long, vulnerable neck. Kurban had bought this necklace for her from the city on her last birthday. It was an inexpensive trinket, but Sohni was very fond of it. Her beating heart was palpitating with a storm. Kurban could not gauge the brilliance of the silent passion of Sohni's obstinate youth.

He wavered.

"But Sohni, if there had been a possibility that you could have kept me in your world, I would not have been able to go anywhere," Kurban said in a faltering voice.

"And now you'll go, you'll leave me, because I cannot get married to you, I cannot keep you in my world, even if I always keep you as the Sultan of my heart! This is not enough for you; isn't that so, Kurban?" Sohni's words, addressing him as 'Kurban', pierced his heart.

He trembled. He stood irresolute. Some words seemed to involuntarily rise from the depths of his heart and clamoured to escape his lips. He could hear the unspoken words in his ears, "No; no; Sohniye, I won't go."

Just then, a sword struck his mother's nape. The bloodied neck fell forward on her chest.... Kurban blanched. Sohni noticed it and drew closer, and Kurban held her hand. Now he had got a firm hold on himself.

"Forgive me, Sohniye, this is beyond my control. I will never become your country's enemy, but I can't stay here either.... Don't forget me!"

Wiping his brimming eyes with Sohni's hand, Kurban kissed it and walked down the stairs. Sohni hoped that he would stop and turn back once. But he descended all the way down the stairs. He didn't look back. He disappeared.

A scream tore through Sohni's heart as she collapsed. Her mother came running and sat down with her in her lap.

"What has happened to my Sohni?"

"Kurban is gone!"

"Where?"

"He's gone to Pakistan!"

"No, Sohni, he won't go!"

"No, Maji, he won't stay!"

"Please control yourself. He's gone to your father's room, I'll persuade him."

"*He won't stay, Maji*—this village is his mother's murderer!" And Sohni began to cry, her hands shielding her eyes.

"Why, Kurban, have you made your decision?" The Sardar asked in an encouraging tone. Tears streamed down Kurban's cheeks. The Sardar clung to him but both were silent for a long time. Maji also came in and hugged Kurban.

"Yes, Bapuji," Kurban wiped his tears and answered. "I have decided! What a stone I have had to place on my heart to take this decision! I won't be able to tell you this, but believe me when I say that you, Maji and Sohni will always remain my world, even if I don't stay in your world."

Sardar had already written the letter. He handed it to Kurban; Kurban touched Maji's feet and then his eyes. Maji clasped him to her bosom and began to cry. Bapuji did not let him touch his feet but shook his hand hard.

Kurban left. He crossed the street. From the window, Sohni saw him leaving.

"But now he won't look back." Sohni sobbed.

He turned the corner.

Translation: Hina Nandrajog

THE DISTANCE TO LAHORE

Surjit Sarna

Standing outside the majestic entrance of the beautiful Guru Nanak Dev University, I asked my husband—

"How far is Lahore?"

"Must be about thirty-five or so kilometres."

"Is that all! Only thirty-five!"

"Yes, only that much. Just about the distance of Dehradun from Mussourie," he added.

Before the creation of Pakistan, it was normal for people to commute between Lahore and Amritsar to and fro from work. Perhaps, it was barely a fifty-five- minute run.

We can go to Mussourie at will, but Lahore...

"It is this very same G.T. Road which takes you to Lahore", my husband pointed out.

Yes, this is the road which goes straight to Lahore—or is it *coming* from there! From that Lahore, the city of my birth, from that very

Lahore, where I spent some beautiful years of my childhood. That very same Lahore which I still visit so often in my dreams—losing myself in the memory of bygone days. It is the same Lahore, which has now become a distant dream.

On reaching the guest house, I lie down heaving a deep sigh without the least desire to say anything. Suddenly, a deep sadness descends upon me. Why is it that we cannot forget? How does one forget! I have had the privilege of growing up in the shade of those trees, those *sibal* trees growing on both sides of the road in Lahore. Often, I have walked to school under their shade. I have lived those seasons.

No one can forget the days of childhood. I don't remember the name of the road on which our house stood, where we lived for a short period—but I remember it was a busy street. Lala Bansidhar's bank was located there and it was the hub of activity. Right across the road was the house of the well-known music director O.P. Nayyar. In those days, he was also a singer.

Almost every day there used to be a gathering there, a *kavi darbar* or something else. And I, young as I was, would very often stand right at the back, behind the crowd, and listen to the speaker or the poet of the evening.

And then I would tell Beji, my *nani*, all about it, and she would scold me, "Don't you go alone. God knows when some firing may take place."

Yes, there was an apprehension in the air, even then I could sense it despite my youth.But the speakers in their criticism of the British rule were daring and courageous. And a large crowd would gather, as if everyone was inspired, moved by the desire to do something. After spending a spell of time in Lahore, we would go back to our parents. Our father, who was in the Military Dairy Farms, was at the time posted at Mhow.

The year was 1944 when I came to Lahore and got admission in the Khalsa College. The college had a school affiliated to it starting right from Class One. It was to this school that I had been admitted and as the exams were approaching, I was fully engrossed in my studies. Prior to joining this school, for about three years, we children had been studying at home under the guidance of a South Indian tutor. And thus, this was the first experience of attending a regular school and it felt very good. The college was pretty spacious and had huge lawns—or at least that was the impression I got at that time. God alone knows how I would react, if I were to see it now. The Principal was one Miss K. Sachdeva, and her friend Miss Satnam was the Vice-Principal. The friendship of Miss Satnam and Miss Hardeep (who taught us English) was a legend in itself. They were room-mates. Later, after Pakistan had come into being, I heard that both had moved to Sidhwan Khurd, though I have no certain information about it. I was envious of their independence and always wondered how lucky they were. One day, I hoped I too would become a teacher and be like them.

I loved the college library best. My hunger for books refused to be satiated. Whatever time I could spare – not spare, but make a special effort to find – I would spend in the library. I would borrow books from the library and back home, after attending to my homework, I would be busy reading well past midnight. The books opened out a whole new world which involved me and I was reluctant to come out of that world.

We – my friends, Kanwaljit, Jasjit, Ratanjit, Khalida and I – would sit in the sun and eat our lunch during recess and discuss the books we had been reading. Kanwaljit Chahal belonged to the royal family of Patiala. She would often tell us about the *mehfil* that was to take place at her home that night and mention that Mallika Pukhraj or some other artist was going to perform. She was studying in Lahore with her mother's sister. And the moment the summers set in, they would leave for Shimla. They lived an aristocratic life right upto the hilt. They had all the appendages of an affluent lifestyle. Jasjit was the daughter of S.P. Chadda. She would always crack jokes which made us laugh a good deal; she was extremely fun loving. The most difficult task we confronted was to construct sentences using proverbs in the Punjabi class. But Jasjit would say, "You are worrying unnecessarily. I'll tell you how simple it is to do so. Just write—*Rani told Shami, 'Neither will there be nine maunds of oil, nor will Radha dance.'* And in the next sentence use Shami for Rani or use Ram and Shyam and it is as simple as that." We followed her advice but the terrible scolding we got after that is something I remember to this day!

All of us were extremely fond of drama, song and music. We would listen to the songs on the radio and then sing them over and over again. Kamala was very good at singing *'Piya milun ko jaana'*[1] and Sudarshan *'Raatan chananiya lang geyian.'*[2] The records of Ramdulari's songs from the film *Chitralekha* were always playing in Kaushalya's room in the hostel.

Enid and Khalida were my special friends, for we kept each other company on the way back home. Enid Shaw's mother was the Head Nurse in the Cantonment Hospital. Whenever we took the local

1 I am to meet my beloved

2 Moonlit nights have passed

bus, I would get off at midpoint and she a little further up. As for Khalida, I have no memory of the direction she took, but she used to wait at the same bus stop as we did. Shimla Hills. That was the name by which the hillock near our college was known. I had never been there, for there was never any time for it; there was always the rush to catch the bus. But everyone used to praise the lovely garden there and even from the bus stop we could see the colourful flowers dancing in the air.

In those days, the wait for the bus was invariably long. We would wait endlessly for the bus. And for this reason, we got to know each other very well. Enid used to sing a song for me at the bus stop, '*Aa bhi jayo aane wale*.'[3] I only recall the first line. And as we whiled away the time singing and listening to songs, the bus would arrive. When I reached home, my older sister's friend Surjit Bhati, my namesake, would invariably be waiting for me. As we drank tea, she would ceaselessly go on chattering with Beji. My sister had got married and Surjit was now my friend. She lived right across, on Infantry Road with her mother's sister who was also the wife of her father's brother. Her parents had abandoned her when she was very young and gone away, God knows where. Since then she had lived with her aunt. She managed the whole house. She was happiest laughing and making others laugh. After about an hour I would walk her back. And as we walked across, invariably there was a comment. Someone would say:

As we talked in the narrow lane your parents got to know
Dragged you away by the hair of your head,
And beat me to death.
Sending you away to your husband's house!

---

3 Come my beloved, I long for you

We would just not look back to find out who this faithful admirer was who stood daily in wait for us. Apparently, he knew a great deal about us, because he would say, "The 'Surjit[2]' are going." We dared not report this to anyone for it would have put an end to the pleasure of our evening walk. So we would merrily laugh amongst ourselves, not mentioning it to anyone else.

Occasionally, on a Sunday morning, we would go to the Regal Cinema to watch an English movie—*David Copperfield* or *Jane Eyre*.

I wonder how we managed to find time to do so many things in addition to our studies! I would be up at four o'clock and study till six and then go back to sleep for another half hour. I would listen to the radio both morning and evening, read novels, go out with friends. Somehow we managed to cram everything into our lives! I was a keen admirer of the artistes who sang from Lahore radio station. Roshanlal Bhatnagar who used to sing, '*Tum ne hum ko bahut sataya, taras jawani par na aaya.*'[4] It was a very popular song as was Vidyanath Seth's '*Lagii dil ki bujhan lun to chale jayega*'[5]. At eleven at night Agha Hashar's plays were often broadcast, and at other times Krishan Chander's *Serai Ki Bahar* or Upendra Nath Ashk's *Anjoo Baji*. Some of these plays were broadcast over and over again.

But our prime favourite was Noor Jehan. She was the queen of Lahore, at least we considered her so. Such a melodious voice, and smiling eyes which twinkled, and a chin with a small cleft as she sang:

Tu kaun si badli mein mere chand hai aaja, taare hain mera
Zakhme jigar
In mein saman jaa

---

4 You have tormented me, showing no mercy for my youth

5 Let me fill my heart's desire before you go

(Behind which cloud are you hiding, my beloved come to me!
The stars are my wounded heart,
Come dwell in them).

And it would move us to tears. And then we read in the newspapers that her brothers had not allowed her to marry; this made us anxious and we fluttered in our helplessness, empathisng with her.

One day we went to see the movie *Ratan* straight from college. In those days in Punjab, there was the system of a 'Ladies Show,' when the tickets were priced at a uniform rate for the whole hall. And it was great fun when there was a crowd of just women and children. We enjoyed ourselves tremendously. How we felt sad for Karan Dewan! How innocent and helpless he was! And as Swaranlata's cousin was a student of our college, she seemed to be one of us.

How carefree were those days! We looked forward eagerly to the Gurupurabs. I don't recall a great deal, but do remember that at night, at the end of the programme there used to be a *kavi darbar* when there were poetry readings. With our handkerchiefs full of shelled nuts, we would move in close to the stage and go on munching them in order to ward off sleep. And when we whispered to each other, the stage secretary would give us a long stare. Once we felt so sleepy that we could not even talk. I was fast asleep. Then Surjit shook me. Perhaps she had herself woken up with a start. She said, "Move away, and stretch your legs." "What?" I asked, uncomprehendingly. "I said, move over, and stretch your legs on the other side." And we burst out into giggles. Then the secretary turned back and warned us, "If you don't quieten down....!" We got really scared and pulled our shawls over our faces.

Ours was a small world but somehow I always had access to new books which opened out other worlds. I would write poems and many a time they were published in *Punjabi Sahitya*. I was an avid reader of Amrita Pritam's poems. In those days Kartar Singh Duggal was the doyen of Punjabi literature. I had read his short story collection *Sver Saar* so many times that everything was sharply etched in my memory.

I longed to see Duggalji, to meet and talk with him. His poetic play was included in his book *Ek Sifar Sifar* (*One Zero Zero*) and we enacted the play *Shohrat di Devi* (*The Lady of Fame*) in which I played the main role. Finally I did meet him one day. Perhaps I told him that I had played the lead in *Shohrat ki Devi* —but it is a vague memory. But I still remember the day. It was winter. Duggalji was talking to someone and laughing quite loudly.

Another literary figure whom I saw at close range was Professor Harcharan Singh who taught in our college. A very good-natured person, he was always smiling and willing to help others—no pretence or false airs. His was a very powerful personality and the role model he provided has always been a constant source of inspiration for me.

But suddenly, there was an explosion. Someone ruthlessly pulled us out of the world of our dreams. Suddenly we grew up.

March 1946 and there were the riots in Pothohar. The flames were bound to reach Lahore. Pamphlets describing all that had happened there reached the gurudwaras. And then one day, Beji told us that the gurudwara people had asked for multiple copies of these pamphlets. Now it became our main occupation, to go on making copies of those pamphlets. May be it was a warning of the troubles to come but now, in retrospect, one can see that they failed to put people on their guard. Was there any gain from all that labour? Only, somewhere, the depths of our souls were traumatised. Everywhere slogans started appearing on the walls of Lahore. "We shall play Holi with blood." But no one took them seriously.

By this time, the possibility of the formation of Pakistan was being talked about everywhere. One heard the same familiar arguments being repeated over and over again: "Governments change but people do not change..." Tension was rising all over the city and on several occasions we had to stay away from classes.

We had Muslim friends in college. Khalida hailed from Jammu. I said to her, "Khalida, don't forget me once Pakistan comes into existence." She began to laugh, "How can I ever forget you?" Her brother-in-law was a Tehsildaar somewhere. Later, I wrote her, God knows, how many letters, and received perhaps a single reply!

As the tension mounted, mohalla committees were constituted. People would keep awake the whole night through. While the men kept watch, the women went up to the terraces with the children. One could see fires flaring up in different parts of the city. We girls wore black suits at night. The shops would remain shut for long periods and when they opened, the streets would overflow with people rushing to buy provisions to store them against an emergency.

Those were dark days, full of fear and uncertainty; there was a constant, nagging fear in the mind. Colleges and schools were closed down. Those days of girlish pleasure, those meetings, were now a thing of the past. There was a time when even a single day without meeting each other made us restless. Now we were not sure of meeting ever again. This fear lurked in some hidden corner of the mind, but none of us had the courage to voice it aloud. The day of the country's division was fast drawing close. All around there was speculation as to who would get Lahore—India or Pakistan. We girls were prisoners in our own homes. The time for the examinations had come and gone but there was no possibility of their being held. The university had been closed ever since the riots began.

I recall that in the month of April there had been a hunger strike in the university and then a firing had taken place, following which schools and colleges had been shut down. That had happened a few months ago. Since then, the summer heat had risen and conditions had deteriorated further.

There was a great restlessness in my heart, the flow of life was no longer free. Our childhood had got lost somewhere. That uncertain period of 1947 and the engulfing darkness had swallowed our all. It had struck at our very souls. Never again did that innocence, the playfulness, that spontaneity return to our lives.

Would we have to leave Lahore—never to return? We repeatedly asked ourselves this rhetorical question. I was extremely attached to Lahore. Even now, as then, I fall in love with places, houses and cities. My friends were there, my college, my studies, and a world all my own—my very own.

But now that individual choice was no longer possible. Whatever had to be done, had to be done collectively. The whole mohalla was one big family. And it was as if we were perpetually standing on live embers unsure of what might happen next. The mohalla had become a tightly-guarded fortress. I felt suffocated and wanted to run away. Before that we had never been so fanatical!

I do remember that during this period, I made a trip to my college. Probably that was my last visit.... Everything was deserted, there was not a person I could see or meet. But, yes, the vendor who sold sweet-potato *chaat* outside the college gate was there. We asked him, "Baba, do you have some *chaat* left?" Yes, he said and slicing the boiled sweet potatoes into small pieces he poured the tamarind chutney over them. But it failed to give me pleasure; it was completely without taste as if a sign of foreboding of hard times to come. Whatever the reason, even one's lips were too tense to smile.

At about this time, one day, there was a huge swelling crowd right at the entry to our street accompanied by a lot of noise and disturbance. Our brother, Inderjit, also rushed out to see what was amiss. On such an occasion, one had no idea as to what was to be done. It appeared as if a group of Muslims was going to attack us. A little later, we saw Jit sitting in a tonga with Bhabiji, my mother, and forging his way towards us. She had come from Bombay, all by herself, in order to fetch us. Not realising how bad the situation actually was she had braved it all alone.

Bhabiji narrated how no tongawallah was prepared to bring her to Dharampura, because in order to reach Dharampura, one had to cross a Muslim colony – Garhi Sahu Di – I don't know how the name has stuck in my memory. But somehow, this half-starved Muslim had agreed to bring her, one cannot say under what compulsion.

Jit was wild at her. How could she act so irresponsibly? It was a miracle that she had come out alive through it all. Everyone voiced the same opinion; but my mother was repeatedly thanking the tongawallah and showering blessings on him, wishing him a long life. "He brought me here at the risk of his own life, these people would have killed him, if Jit had not reached there on time."

The tongawallah was trembling with fear, today he had had a close shave with death! We brought him upstairs and gave him a drink of water. He was like an angel for us and my grandmother blessed him, his family, his children and his kind from the depths of her heart. My mother took out two hundred rupees and gave them to him. Comforting him she said, "Don't be scared, brother. Now someone will escort you to your place safe and sound. Don't be afraid."

And finally my brother Jit along with three or four other men from the mohalla accompanied him as far as Garhi Sahu Di. This was what Lahore was like in those days – an anxious, fearful and apprehensive Lahore; a Lahore on fire, a city of broken as well as honoured friendships, a Lahore of gatherings and get-togethers, of meetings – the city of my childhood, my birthplace Lahore!

Why was it changing? What wrong had we done that we were being made to suffer the consequences of the wrong decisions of our leaders? Our generation has borne this tragedy of history! I will never forget you Lahore, I'll never forget you. And I again ask my husband: "How far is Lahore?" and then not waiting for a reply go on, "I don't know how far it is or how near. One Lahore lives in my heart, close to me and there is another one, far away, in an alien land."

Translation: Jasbir Jain

COME, SISTER FATIMA

Baldev Singh

I am spring-cleaning the house as I do every year just before Diwali. I drag superfluous things out of the house to the courtyard. I want to make full use of Sunday. I have also managed to get the children to cooperate. They enjoy dragging out old shoes, empty bottles, used school books and notebooks, threadbare plastic webbing tape, defunct tubes, switches, broken toys, old bicycle tyres, and a whole lot of other junk. This is as engrossing as any game as far as they are concerned. I am amazed! God knows how much trash Bebe has thrown inside the store. "They may come in useful someday," she says to everyone.

Today Bebe is probably visiting someone in the neighbourhood, otherwise she would have got annoyed at this misdemeanour. She would have picked up sundry things and asked us, "Why are you throwing this? And this shoe? This is still in good condition. Does anyone ever discard toys that one's children have played with? Only the fortunate ones have these things...."

Things are piled haphazardly in the courtyard like a second-hand goods shop. The wife has emptied out the bag of dried up rotis from the kitchen. "Throw out these as well," she said, turning up her nose at the fungus-infested rotis. The children come, heaving under the weight of Bebe's old spinning wheel that has been partially eaten by termites. "Let's get rid of this rubbish too," I think. In the past 20-25 years I have never seen Bebe spinning on it. But she dusts it occasionally. Sometimes she even murmurs little nothings to it, as if it were made of flesh and bone. But I know that all its joints and hinges are loose.

Now I hope a scrap-collector will come along before Bebe returns. But what I fear happens. Bebe's walking stick comes tapping on the paved ground into the courtyard, and she looks at the scattered heap with astonishment, "What are you up to, son?"

I look at Bebe like a thief caught red-handed.

"And why have you brought this out?" A distressed look appears on mother's face. "Is this to be discarded?" She looks at the spinning wheel with affection. Her eyes moisten. I feel that Bebe is hurt. But instead of owning up to shame, I ask in an irritated tone, "Bebe, what will you do with this? You have never spun a thing."

"No, son. So what if I have never spun anything? It doesn't mean that we should throw it out of the house. I haven't done any work for the past ten years either. I haven't cooked a meal; never cleaned the place. Have you thrown me out?" Bebe's argument silences me. "What do you know about this? This is something that I hold in trust for Fatima. I will never let it go as long as I am alive. You can do what you like with it once I'm dead," announces Bebe, and pulls the spinning wheel out of the littered heap, beginning to croon softly to it.

I look at Bebe and the spinning wheel by turn. The spindle is bent. The string that turns the spindle is missing altogether. As far as physical conditions go, Bebe is little better than the spinning wheel. Her knees ache, the teeth are missing, and her eyesight is very weak.

"You were a baby at that time. About three-four years old." Bebe begins to look at the past fifty years through the spinning wheel. "I remember every bit of it. It was about sunset when Fatima came crying to our house. She said, 'Oh, my dear, I've heard the nation has become free. And Pakistan has been created. We'll have to go there. My Abba and Chacha are already packing our things.' It was as if I stopped breathing. Fatima wouldn't stop crying. She was crying and speaking simultaneously, 'Sister, how will we leave these lanes, this village, this house, these lands, this country? God knows what sort of people live there? I've not even spent two days at my maternal grandparents' place. I get bored without you. What will I do now?'"

I gape at Bebe's choked voice. Bebe is looking far away.

"Here, Bebe, are you crying?" I ask, surprised.

Bebe sighs and attempts a weak laugh. "What else do I have left except tears? It has been fifty years since then, but it seems to have happened yesterday. She gave me this when she left. She used to say that it was dearer to her than sons. If you had been any older at that time you would have seen how the spinning wheel seemed to talk. The pole of the spinning wheel seemed to keep time with our tunes...." Bebe heaves a sigh. Wipes her eyes. But they fill up again. "She kept caressing it when she left. She said, 'Who knows, the nations may become one again? Then I'll come to take my spinning wheel back....' What could one say to someone leaving like this? Leaving behind all ancestral possessions...!"

Bebe speaks softly to herself. God knows whether she is talking to the spinning wheel or to Fatima. I do not wish to disturb Bebe at such an emotional moment. I hush the children with silent gestures. They are really excited. They examine the things by turning them all over and upside down. But when they drop something, they steal an apprehensive look at Bebe and me and place their fingers on their lips and motion to each other to keep quiet.

The scrap-collector has come. Bebe is holding on to the spinning wheel as if she is afraid of it being snatched away.

The scrap-collector has scavenged all the odds and ends. These people are marvellous. They make a living out of things that we consider junk. Now the scrap-collector stands aside to calculate the price. How much iron, how many bottles, how much broken glass, how much plastic and waste paper.... Different materials carry different prices.

Bebe is still dusting and cleaning the spinning wheel. "Son, there was so much killing then.... Oh my God! People became worse than beasts. Utterly wild like animals. The Muslims were still inside their homes. Our people began to loot their houses, began to set their houses on fire. Drove their cattle into their own pens...."

"Didn't the Muslims fight back, Bebe?" I ask.

"How could they fight, son? The very people they trusted were the leaders of the looting and killing mobs. The Muslims threw down their heads in humiliation like sheep. There was an open space in front of our house in our village; all the Muslims were herded there."

"They say the Muslims killed a lot of our people on the other side."

"They must have, son. What we did to them, they must have done to us. The animal is within man. Only the horns are invisible!" Bebe's face indicates that she is looking at the burning houses at the time of Partition in 1947.

The scrap-collector sums up the amount and hands over the money. I place this money before Bebe. Bebe is watching the groaning-moaning multitudes of people crawling before her with sad, brimming eyes. "No, son. What will I do with money? But son, don't throw this spinning wheel of mine. Fatima! God knows where she would be now! She was dearer to me than my own sister. She must be thinking, "My spinning wheel is there. The countries might have been divided, but our love hasn't been severed.' I met her in my dream yesterday. No one can stop that, can they?"

I have read a lot about 'freedom achieved at the stroke of midnight'. But Bebe seems to be living out an agonising facet of that reality.

"Here, Bebe, let me put it back in the house or you won't stop crying!" I want Bebe to come out of the past.

"Son! How would you feel if someone drags you out of a prosperous home and tells you to go wherever you like, but never to come back! Today people might wonder how that is possible. But I have seen it happen," sighs Bebe. I drag the spinning wheel inside.

A few days later, we decided to get the house whitewashed and the doors and windows painted. I found a labourer for the job and gave him the contract after explaining the scope of the work. I would pay him for his labour and provide the material myself. If one employs them on daily wages, then they dawdle, never getting around to finishing the job. They take an hour just to drink a cup of tea. If one gives the work on contract, then they work like the devil. They don't stop working even after dark. One has to ask them to stop. But one has to keep an eye on them during the contract. They try to get away with shoddy work.

In just about three days, the men finish the whitewashing and begin painting the doors and windows. I give them instructions when I leave for work—"This house is being painted for the first time since we came to the city from the village. Please do the work thoroughly. Don't paint over the rust." They promise me, "Yes, rest assured...all right." But according to my wife they do exactly as they please. "After every hour they say—'Some tea, Bibiji.' I haven't ever seen them eat in the break," she says exasperatedly.

One day when I return I see Bebe getting her spinning wheel painted by the labourer. She is sitting beside him. The labourer is also very happy. Now these people have learnt some stratagems. Bebe does not like to see me return; I can gauge this from her face. The glow on her face as she had watched the spinning wheel being painted has faded. Perhaps Bebe fears that I'll be angry.

"There was some extra paint. I thought it would go waste, so let's use it on the spinning wheel," Bebe offers justification.

"Bebe, you have never used it. Nor will it ever work." I show my annoyance.

"It will work, son, it will." There is quiet determination writ large on Bebe's face.

"You are wasting their time unnecessarily."

"A half an hour won't make any difference. See how beautiful it looks. As if Fatima has given it to me just now!" The lustre is back on Bebe's face.

The labourer brings all the colours he has. He is also enjoying himself. Bebe tells him, "It belongs to my friend. Now she is in Pakistan. God knows if she is alive or not."

"Then I will not charge a penny. Just give me another cup of tea," the labourer says when he sees the sadness on Bebe's face.

At times I feel that there is humanity in the labourer. At other times I feel that he is a trickster. He makes arrangements for his needs by appearing to be very simple and sweet. My wife also says, "He is really very simple, poor soul. He's left his country. He has no one here." But I know that these labourers chuckle among themselves when they recount how they have fooled people.

The labourer has displayed great artistry and polished the spinning wheel beautifully. Now he places it in the sun. Bebe is watching it from a distance. Although it is decrepit now, it appears to be new.

Bebe's daughters-in-law turn up their noses at the spinning wheel and Bebe. They nudge each other. Bebe understands everything but says nothing.

"Now Bebe will spin cotton," the younger daughter-in-law says loudly to her older counterpart, in Bebe's hearing.

"We will give the contract of weaving sheets and *durries* for our daughter's wedding only to Bebe." The younger one laughs heartily at this.

"The sum total of all the knowledge you have in your bellies, I have in my nails alone. I know you very well." There is anger and indignation on Bebe's face.

"Bebe we are only talking about your spinning wheel as old as Independence. Why are you quarrelling with us?" The younger daughter-in-law is in the mood for appeasement, but does not sound very conciliatory.

"Go away. What do you know about the meaning of Independence? You only believe in eating, drinking and making merry!" Bebe is more irritated.

I know that if her daughters-in-law don't keep quiet Bebe can even go into a frenzy of anger. I go and tell them to mind their own business.

They leave but the younger one ripostes as she goes, "We'll see what Bebe spins on this spinning wheel."

"Let the paint dry, then I'll show you how I can spin. Hasn't been born yet, and look at her talk!" Bebe's face flashes a challenge.

The paint-work is complete. The peculiar odour of paint that pervades the house is pleasant. One feels proud of the clean and tidy house.

The paint on the spinning wheel is dry now.

But what is this? Bebe has again fetched the spinning wheel that has been kept carefully wrapped in a *khes*[1] inside. She looks at me and says, "Do these women let me rest?" Her pointed remark is addressed to her daughters-in-law.

The latter smirk and snicker.

"An ascetic came to beg at the door. They say, 'He must have heard the sound of my spinning wheel.' Today I'll show them."

The daughters-in-law laugh again.

"How will you spin now, Bebe? The spinning wheel is in no better condition than you are." The younger daughter-in-law is forever teasing her.

"Spinning is an art. What would you know about it?" Bebe is not one to accept defeat easily.

Her face reflects determination, she has long years of experience and she takes pride in her friend's spinning wheel.

Bebe sits on a stool and oils the joints. She puts in a new string. She oils the connecting pole. Then she spins it to straighten the bent spindle. With a slight pressure of her finger she straightens

1 Khes: A thick cotton blanket

the spindle. Then she brings out some cotton saved up from some distant past.

The daughters-in-law are watching her movements and laughing. But Bebe is absolutely serious.

Bebe first tests the empty spinning wheel by giving it a twirl. Everything seems to be fine. Then she takes a little ball of cotton and twists it with her hands. Before bringing the cotton in contact with the spindle she shuts her eyes and meditates for a while and then says softly, "Come, Sister Fatima, let us spin!"

When Bebe twirls the wheel and swings her left hand backwards after touching it to the head of the spindle, a thin long thread is visible for all to see. The daughters-in-law watch, agape. They cover their open mouths with their hands in surprise.

Bebe spins on, eyes streaming.

Translation: Hina Nandrajog

THE MAN WHO REFUSED TO DIE

Ahmed Salim

What is this? What is happening to me? Why is everything suddenly looming so large? Or is it that I'm shrinking in size? Only last month I celebrated my twenty-sixth birthday; why then do I suddenly look like a young child? And my room, with the bust of Buddha in the cornice and the picture of Bhagat Singh, my hero, why is it suddenly going up in smoke?

Where am I? What is this forest? Just a moment ago I was in my room reading *Heer* and thinking of my own beloved, but now…I stand forsaken in this forest. How can this be possible?

And who is this old man coming towards me from the trees? From the looks of him he could be either a philosopher or an absconder from the law. "Who are you? And what are you doing here?" he asks me.

What shall I say? What will he think if I tell him the truth? Surely, he will think I have gone mad. Or else been kidnapped, abandoned, or lost. But how did it come about?

The old man comes nearer, touches me at the shoulder and asks, "Have you lost your way?"

I stand dumbfounded.

"Do you want to find your way out of here?" the old man asks again.

What can I say? Which road leads back to my study, to my lost youth? What is this waking nightmare?

"Say something, my child," the old man says with sympathy and concern.

"I have lost my twenty-six years," I blurt out.

"Twenty-six years?" The old man looks at me and smiles. "Twenty-six years. Come, let us search for them together. But are you sure you can recognise them?"

"My features resemble my mother's but the features of my lost years resemble those of my dead grandfather," I tell him.

"I see," says the old man. Then, leading me by the hand, he starts walking through the forest, waving aside the thick branches with one sweep of his hand.

"We are passing through history," he says, "and these leaves are the innumerable pages of its book."

"But I can't read anymore!" I exclaim helplessly.

"Yes, that is bound to happen. Wherever there is oppression there exists a dark forest between the past and the present. But as one strides onwards this darkness becomes clear."

I look at the old man as though I understand what he says.

"Where does this forest end?" I ask him impatiently.

"Don't worry. We have passed the darker years; your youth must be somewhere nearby. Are you sure you can recognise it?"

"Of course. How could I forget it? The scars of two wars, the ravages of hunger for food and for my love. I can never forget it," I say.

The forest ends abruptly. We stand facing a city. I see the winding turrets of the many mosques. The noise of the city bursts upon my senses.

"You have lost recognition of your years. Beware, they lurk somewhere around. Somewhere here…" And then the old man falls silent.

I'm back to my city! Its streets full of filth and dried blood! Angry graffiti screams on its dilapidated walls. Twenty-six years ago, a young girl screamed as she brought me forth into the world, into the domain of this city. That girl later became old. Oh my poor, poor mother!

"Keep your eyes open," says the old man as we pass through the narrow lanes. On the walls I notice 'Wanted Dead or Alive' posters. The old man points to them and says,

"Do you see these posters? They are for me. The government wishes to hang me."

I shudder. "You? No, no. That can't be possible. Why don't you hide?"

"Don't worry, my son. History can never be concealed." The old man is now showing me pages from my past. My childhood, my schooldays. My mother, our lives of constant need and helplessness. Riots, blood, youth, belief in struggle, agitation. The Kot Lakhpat prison…

"I resemble all those who are wanted dead or alive for 'subversive activities'. They have hanged me twenty-five times over, yet I refuse to die."

I peer at the old man. He does have some resemblance to my grandfather. I make a point of telling him so.

"You have mentioned your grandfather before. Who is he?" He asks.

"Not is, but was. They killed him."

"Why?"

"He started a movement to stop army recruitment from his area. He stood firm when they came to get him, and he said, 'I shall not even let a dog from my beloved land go with you, leave alone my people.' He was shot dead on charges of inciting people against the state."

There is a noise around us. It sounds like police whistles. Dogs bark. The old man quickly disengages his hand from mine.

"Go, hide," he orders me. "You were released just yesterday. This time they will get me." The old man pushes me towards a dark corner and moves away. I stand there speechless and watch them pounce on him from all sides and clap handcuffs on him. He holds his head high as they lead him away, and he walks away with dignity. I jump to stop them but my eye is caught by the writing on the wall. It reads:

WANTED
DEAD OR ALIVE
WARIS SHAH

Waris Shah has been hanged 25 times already and the police are still searching for him! His crime was to have been born in the undivided Punjab. The land now stands partitioned but this man's spirit is not. If caught dead or alive, a handsome reward awaits the man who turns him in.

My head begins to reel, I feel as if everything around me is crumbling, everything going up in smoke. Yes, I feel my height increasing. Yes, I am back in my room with the Buddha and Bhagat Singh and *Heer*. The book lies open in my lap, the pages wet with tears. But whose tears? Tears for whom?

I am searching for the answer.

Translation: The Author

BLACK WATERS, DARK WELL

Keki Daruwalla

We could easily have gone through life without ever meeting again. But in the North my name is not easily forgotten. It sticks like a leech to the memory cells of others.

So when we were introduced at a party, he zeroed in on me across forty years. The years peeled away like old bark. Gurpreet had been my elder brother's contemporary in school. His younger brother Harpreet and I were in the same class in Arya School, Lyallpur. Harpreet had pushed off to Canada where he had made good (who hasn't?) and had eventually got to own a farm of five hundred acres. When he saw my eyes pop out he told me he owned a farm in Karnal and though he had no more than a hundred acres to himself, much of it through *benami* transactions, he had turned it into a fine place. He called it the Balbir Ranch, after his grandfather. Ranch? Trust, Gurpreet, I thought.

As we clinked glasses at the party, (our host was a corporate honcho) I asked him about his beautiful sister whose name had slipped my memory. What could it be, Satinder or Maninder or

Kulwinder? More than fifty per cent chance of an 'Inder' being there at the end of it. What Indra, king of Devtas, had to do with Sikh women had always foxed me. Why couldn't they be named after goddesses or apsaras? And why did Indra always have to be mispronounced as Inder? There was also the intriguing possibility that a Pushpinder Singh could be married to a Pushpinder Kaur, a Rajinder Singh getting hooked to a Rajinder Kaur. What would happen then?

He heard my question but didn't answer. Instead he smiled the kind of smile where the lips go fissuring across the cheeks and then settle back, like two rubber bands being stretched a little and then falling back in place. We went into a quiet huddle for a while, just sipping from our glasses. He asked me about my brothers and I said they were fine. He asked me about Jal in particular and I told him he was dead. Also told him how we had kept the news from our by then semi senile mother, right till she died five years later.

"Didn't she ask about him?"

"She did, till the end, though she was in such a haze that she hardly recognised her other sons."

"My grandmother died and we too kept something from her. I'll tell you about it when we meet next."

We bumped into each other in Delhi again. He kept coming for his mother's treatment. He would also land up at the Gymkhana Club once a year when elections to the executive committee were held. Each time the invitations to the farm were renewed and each time I said I'd definitely turn up.

Meanwhile whenever I thought of Gurpreet, that twenty-minute silence that had descended on him when I had asked him about his sister troubled me. Over the years her face came back, fair and oval and beautiful, and her lithe step as she played hopscotch, and seven tiles with us boys. It was only hockey we wouldn't let her play with us, much to her chagrin—for it would have been a blow to our male pride if she had scored a goal.

Some work cropped up at Chandigarh and I decided to drop in on Gurpreet at Karnal. One winter morning I found myself at the Balbir Ranch—low-roofed, sleek and air conditioned. We got down to exchanging notes, if an exchange it could be called, because for me Lyallpur was almost beyond recall. I faintly recalled our house on Race Course Road, though I remember it also on Jail Road, for what good reason, I can't tell. We had an earlier house which I can't recall—except for the landlord's name, Fazldin, and a big mulberry tree in the compound. We used to go out playing hockey against boys from Chinot Bazar and Kutchery Bazar. I remember two dogs, one big and brown called Timmy who belonged to Dr. Shri Ram. He got poisoned by Municipal workers. The other was a Spotty, a fellow with black spots on a white hide who belonged to a dignified Christian gentleman, Isa Das.

In the evening as we sat down for a drink in his lawn. I took my usual whiskey. Gurpreet prepared his drink elaborately, vodka and tomato juice, the glass-rim lined with salt. I asked him what he had kept from his grandmother, whom the family called Bijee.

"It was Balwinder's death," he answered. Ah, so that was the name. Of course I remembered now. We used to call her Balli (If Ali had another 'l' to the name it would have rhymed with Balli.) Her face floated into sight, smooth, oval and fair. We talked far into the night. The next day, despite a nagging headache, I pieced together the following.

With the early summer of '47 turning ugly – though no one had guessed as yet how ugly – Sardar Gursharan Singh, Gurpreet's father decided to send the women of the house off to his father-in-law's place, a few miles to the east of Sialkot. Lyallpur was proving troublesome, what with the Sikhs turning defiant under the exhortations of Master Tara Singh. A huge procession generously sprayed with spear-wielding Nihangs, had wound its slow serpentine way through the stunned bazaars, shouting anti-Pakistan slogans. That was bound to bring in further trouble, thought his father. So it fell to Gurpreet's lot on his first assignment as an adult to escort his mother and Balwinder to Sialkot. The protests from the matriarch were loud and fierce. Sikh women were not prepared to leave their husbands in a hot spot and flee to safety. Their forebodings were intuitive and much nearer the mark than the misplaced optimism of their male kin. Gursharan overrode the objections. So the train to Lahore and then one to Sialkot, where Gurpreet left sister and mother to the cares of his grandfather Sardar Balbir Singh, who had come in his black Chevrolet to the station. He had also brought his tonga for the baggage, along with two retainers sporting their single barrel twelve bore guns. I envied Gurpreet his vivid recall.

Balbir Singh had a sizeable chunk of land fed by the waters of the Upper Chenab Canal, just a few miles North-West of Chaprara. His lands were the envy of rival zamindars, none more than Rai Bahadur Satnam Singh's, whose forefathers had helped the British during the Mutiny and were rewarded with jagirs. Unfortunately for Satnam Singh, the network of canals had not come up then. So his lands were not well irrigated, as Balbir Singh's more modest holdings. Over the generations the rivalry had become bitter, though it had seldom flared into open hostility.

"Things started getting worse in Punjab", Gurpreet continued his tale. Each morning apparently brought a new rumour. Even Gurdaspur seemed to be going to Pakistan. "I hope they don't walk away with Delhi" Balbir Singh would mutter rather disconsolately. His tone had turned subdued. He didn't want his daughter and granddaughter to be party to his fears. He had no son and his lands would go to his daughter. He was damned if he was ever going to migrate once this Hindustan-Pakistan business was over. A zamindar died where his lands were, where his wheat grew and his mustard flowered and his gram sprouted, where each serf and retainer belonged to you and everyone knew you—from the village idiot to the moorhen. Relatives across the border were asking him to come away. Balbir wouldn't budge. He was fond of a particular Punjabi saying:

Jo sukh chajju de chubare
Na Balkh, na Bukhare.

Neither Balkh nor Bukhare could give you the happiness of home.

After three months of alarms and excursions, of contrary rumours sweeping the plains...after three months during which dreams themselves turned noisy with the clang of conflict...after a summer of passions which the rains did nothing to cool came the fateful day. According to Gurpreet, sixty hours after the tragedy, two hours before sunrise the great zamindar left his lands watered by the Chenab and slunk away in his black Chevrolet. His Muslim retainers and peasants helped him, running alongside his car on the dirt road till he reached the border. Some of them carried headloads for him, his gramophone, books and bric-a-brac. At the crack of dawn, with the sun flaring behind the *sarkanda* reeds, they crossed the border.

Gurpreet put his vodka glass down with finality. I suddenly became conscious of the staccato speech of the crickets. The entire night seemed a-bristle with their chirp. We moved in, for it had turned cold, had our dinner and then sat in the veranda over coffee.

"Gurpreet, if Balli died in Sialkot, surely her grandmother would have known!" I objected.

"Didn't I tell you that when we went to Sialkot we found Bijee had already been packed off to her sister's place in Hoshiarpur? That is how this cat-and-mouse game started with the old lady. We told her that Balli had been admitted to a medical college in the South. It was one of those off-the-cuff lies we were hard put to stick to. She would want to knit pullovers for Balli—perhaps someone had inadvertently mentioned Ooty. The more you embellish a lie the more pitfalls you face. We told her the South had no winter. Why so far, she asked. "Couldn't you put her in some college nearby? *Thwadi mat maari gayee see*?" (Did you take leave of your senses?) But Dad told her that they had sent Balli off to the South so that the riots and chaos in the North did not affect her psychologically.

"Next summer she was agitated again. Why hasn't Balli come? Where could we have brought her, we shot back. We still did not have a proper house. We were tenants in a poky little flat in West Patel Nagar. It was two years later that we bought some land here in Karnal with some of the gold that grandfather had brought with him. Of course Father put in a lot of his own money.

"Then the grand old slightly tyrannical man of the upper Chenab died of a stroke and the old woman stopped eating. A few months later she broke her thighbone in a fall. All at once she started losing her hold on memory.

"You can't live with a lie too long. Mum and dad even thought of visiting some fatal disease on poor Balli and later announcing her 'departure.' Fortunately they changed their mind. Even in her semi lucid state she would have seen through the game. Death can't be feigned, it arrives with telegrams and mourners, breast beating and professional mourners.

"Moreover she would not be around too long, so where was the point hurting her? As it is she was plagued with disorienting dreams. She had started of late seeing the well in her old Chaprara farm. Forgetfulness can make you a bit of a saint. You forget what is yours and what belongs to others. Commodities get reduced to commodities—neither mine nor yours. (This guy Gurpreet was becoming a philosopher). She would take off an ornament and give it away to a servant maid. Gurpreet's mum would snatch back the gift. She saw to it that the ornaments Bijee wore were lightweight. One day she gave away an eighteen carat gold ring topped by a cheap sapphire. That night Bijee heard Balli's voice echoing and re-echoing in their old well at Chaprara. Nothing symbolises memory better than a well, its waters dark, its wall pulsing with echoes. Anything circular signifies oneness. (Gurpreet seemed to be going over the top now, I thought). Both draw on things subterranean; both are stained with the dark.

'The next morning Bijee heard the serving maid wailing and tearing her hair. She had dropped her ring while drawing water from the well. The ranch had not come up by then and they were living like any other in the village. When Bijee heard that wail some thing clicked in her brain through all the fog of the dreams swirling around her. And she said, "It is not just the ring that has fallen into the well. Balli is also lying there."

I let the whole thing sink in. Then I thought to myself that I simply had to stay another day here. Twenty-four hours were not enough. During the day we went around on Gurpreet's tractor, travelled by jeep alongside acres and acres of sunflower, even went into the smelly chicken coop, which was clucking away. In the evening as we sat down to our drink I asked the question I had been mulling over. He hadn't said a word about how Balli died.

Difficult question—there's nothing about death which is simple. For about ten minutes, silence lay between us like a river, something tangible and fluent that flowed between and separated us. I also felt that he was trying to staunch the bleeding memory of his sister's death.

"I have mentioned Satnam Singh to you, haven't I?"

I nodded.

"Well he and Grandpa hated each other; that also you know perhaps. Satnam had a grandson, Gurbaksh by name. Balli and I would sometimes sneak away and play with him, but never in the knowledge of my grandfather. He would have chewed us up if he had come to know. A young girl would have liked to put her arms around the slender trunk of Gurbaksh. He was maybe two years older than Balli and they started going around. Balbir Singh saw them together one day. His face turned dark. '*Mundaiya*' (boy) he said, '*Khabardar* if I see you on my lands again! It won't go well with you.'

"And that was that till Satnam Singh came over one day on his chestnut mare, bristling with anger. '*Oye* Khabardar Singh! When will you stop threatening children and start looking people of your age in the eye?'

"Balbir Singh kept his cool though his chest heaved with anger. 'I will not say anything in answer. You are on my estate and I refuse to be discourteous.'

"Satnam shot back: 'But while talking to that grandson of mine you forgot your manners!'

"Balbir restrained himself even in the face of further taunts right till the time Satnam Singh turned his mare round and rode off. Their exchange had been heard by all and sundry. Both landlords had flunkies living off their lands. They started flexing their muscles and hurling abuse at each other. The situation was moving towards a showdown."

"Fear is a terrible thing," continued Gurpreet. "It shackles you. But if passion is around, it removes the shackles and leads you by the nose. The congealed blood suddenly thaws and the feet are not even aware that they were frozen into immobility just a while ago. Who knows the roots of passion?" asked Gurpreet rhetorically. "Who knows anything about the match that ignites it all? What turns a boy on? Perhaps just a shy smile or the way a girl shakes her head and the braids toss around till she holds them in her hand and plays with them till they fall across her breasts. What gives a girl the hots? How would I know? Perhaps the way hair slants across his forearm, or the way he gets gooseflesh as her hand brushes against his. Or perhaps just that slim hard waist she wants to get her arms around, or the fuzz on his chin, or the strength in his arm as he propels her through a door. What makes the blood tingle and the hand turn nervous with perspiration? There can't be answers to all this.

"What it all boils down to is that a boy and a girl in the first flush of passion can't really be kept apart by gates or walls. So Gurbaksh and Balli met that fateful evening. It was a large house and Balli had a room to herself. The boy must have slipped in somehow. Balbir Singh's estate was old style, with a well surrounded by shrubbery, a yoke of oxen, a hitching post for a horse which Balbir Singh was almost too old to ride…they were all there. So were the two love birds possibly hovering around the well."

But there were things other than love brewing in the countryside.

"The tree of hate was leafing," said Gurpreet. It was not just the flunkies of Satnam and Balbir who were spouting venom and reaching for each other's throats. There were also creatures called Muslims and Sikhs, not forgetting the Hindus. A mob of Muslims from Chak Kaley Khan and other villages in the west came raging towards the estates of these two Sardars. And there were the doughty Dogras from Ranbir Singh Pura and Suchetgarh and areas south of Rane Chak who already knew of the Muslim onslaught. Such information was carried on the wind's back those days. You had only to sniff the air and you knew what was going to happen. That's clairvoyance for you—reduced to wind-sniffing. The Dogras came with stave and scythe and spear. Blood flowed, but not as it could have flowed. Each side saw how well prepared the enemy was. Hence it was more of skirmishing than a pitched battle. When mobs run they sound like stampeding herds. And there was much running around and shouting—challenge and curse and abuse, the entire veneer of bravado to cover a thick layer of fear.

These two kids must have thought – I am only guessing – that the entire fight was over them and their feelings for each other, possibly even this after-dusk meeting near the well. Whether it was terror which made them take this step or guilt, one doesn't know. That a Hindu-Muslim or Sikh-Muslim fracas was raging around them and taking its toll did not occur to them perhaps.

When the dust and the mobs had disappeared, they found Balli missing. Gurbaksh could not be located either, by Satnam's people. They searched everywhere and drew a blank.

Finally they looked into the well.

A BUNCH OF NARCISSUS

Surjit Sarna

Dear Lahore,

I am writing to you after a long time.... I wrote many letters to you earlier, but received no response...I've heard that you've changed a great deal. Perhaps, now you may not even recognise us! Do you ever think about us? Though, it doesn't seem possible that you would forget us....

I have a feeling that even if thousands of people settle on your vast and picturesque plains, lending colour and life to the environment, you would still cherish the memories of our childhood, spent in your lanes and by-lanes...

I seem to lose myself in the shadowy forests of my memories. It is with great difficulty that I scramble on to the right path which always leads to you. Flinging open the doors and the casements of the windows shuttered and closed years ago, with my tears and sighs, I try to clear the cobwebs away and wipe off the dust of time which lies thick on everything.

I'm very restless today. You seem to be haunting my memories... do you know why? A letter lies before me, a letter written by my son Navtej's son, which he wrote to Greater Kailash—

'Dear Greater Kailash,

I think of you and remember you a great deal! Lots of love—'

That is all. But after I read this letter a twinge of pain shot through me, an intense and inexpressible pain rent my heart. What Greater Kailash is to Satyajit, you were to me, my dear Lahore. For me, you are still mine, though more than five decades have gone by. Sometimes it seems as if aeons have passed since we parted from you. And then, it seems that it was only yesterday....It was our own city, and those were our own gullies and mohallas...that school... the first day at the college...the group of friends, those lovely, lively evenings...where have they all gone? Punjab lay wounded and bleeding, and no remedy could be found to staunch its gaping wounds. And we saw and lived through the horror of those days at such a tender age!

The hateful shadows of those riots have seeped into my soul, and even now, when I think of those days, I am engulfed by the desolation of that anguish...

What golden days were those...we friends would all get together and go out. Whenever we were late, I would beg my friend Surjit— "Drop me first...come home with me!" She would laugh and she and Shabnam would accompany me home. Shabnam was her friend, and they were both actually my elder sister's friends. When she had got married they had taken me into their circle of friendship.

Shabbo, where are you now? I have had no news of you. I hope that you are reading this letter. You may seem to be far away, but in my mind you have always been with me. You may not be aware of this. You also would not have forgotten those days. This is the truth…

Those days, when we would all gather at Surjit's home in the evening…their home would be full of life. Her uncle had three sons – Satbir, Hardeep and Balbir – and they were full of fun and cheer! She would trail behind them, picking up things that they left scattered all over. Surjit's parents were dead and she lived with her uncle and aunt. Her aunt (*chachi*) also happened to be her mother's sister.

Shabnam…we all called you Shabbo with love…your beautiful image still dazzles me…fair of complexion with large dark lovely eyes, your colourful *chunni* flung across your shoulders, invariably slipping off all the time. In those days, I was reading *Heer* – the famous love legend of Punjab – for the first time, and Shabbo…to me you seemed to be the personification of Heer! I was very fond of you, and at the first opportunity I would rush to your house. Any time at all I got to myself I wanted to spend with you.

Many Muslim families lived around us. Perhaps those days the difference between Hindu and Muslim was not so sharp.

Satbir had, by then, joined the Indian Air Force. Their home was always filled with laughter. He was a fun-loving man. Whenever I was with them, I didn't want to come away. I forgot that I had to study and Beji would be angry. All I wanted was to sit there with them.

Satbir would always tease me… he called me "Buddhu", "Pagal". Sometimes, his teasing made me cry, but he never behaved like this with you…the days you did not come to their home, he would beg me—"Jiti, go; please go and bring Shabbo with you…"

"I? How can I go?" I pretended to be busy. "Why can't you go? Is there mehandi on your feet? Let me see…" and despite my telling him not to, he would touch my feet and would say—"Be sensible for once!"

If I complained to Surjit, he would call me, *"Roni billi"* (the cat who cries), and when I would come over to fetch you, you also took your own time and came grudgingly. The moment you arrived…he would forget all about me. You would both be absorbed in each other…both of you, and Surjit would also join you. I was the only one left outside the charmed circle! Often, I interrupted you but that hardly made a difference. And I'd leave you to help Surjit with the cooking.

Sometimes, Satbir took us all to the movies. I still remember the day the three of us had reached the cinema and Satbir was waiting for us – the movie was *Sikander*. Prithviraj Kapoor was the hero and Vanmala the heroine. During the film the two of you kept talking and I and Surjit sat isolated, a little cut off. All the pleasure drained away. I could not fathom why I was so restless. It was nothing except the naiveté of a foolish heart! Perhaps this happens to all of us, at some time or the other in our lives.

Days were slipping away…Shabbo do you remember? I still remember the winter rains in Lahore…It was bitterly cold, and during the day we all used to assemble at the Simla Hills bus stop, and sitting on the damp grass, talk and sing for hours! We have received so much love from the soft caressing breeze of Lahore, which still blows fresh across its roads and lanes.

So many meetings! So many 'meals' and kite flying sessions! It was a hectic time politically and there were many literary meetings, poetic sessions, *kavi* durbars for budding poets…. Somehow or the other I would find my way to those poetic assemblies and political gatherings. You and Surjit gave me no support at those meetings.

Then Satbir went away for his training. I asked him to get me a length of air- force blue serge. When he came back from his training, he did bring the material for me!

It was the winter of 1946. I had expected Satbir to personally bring over the material to me, but nothing of that sort happened. Yet, I gave the serge to the tailor to be made into a coat.

Our exams were drawing near, but Satbir was still on leave, and who had the time to study? That day should still be fresh in your mind, when we had gone shopping at Anarkali. I was wearing my new coat. When I put it on for the first time and had asked Surjit and Satbir, "How does my coat look?" Satbir had not even glanced at me. With only a fleeting glance in my direction he had muttered— "Good!"

"It is good, but how does it look on me?" I persisted.

His eyes, however, were fixed on your black *chunni* which had got entangled with your thick plaits. It was Surjit who had answered with a laugh—"It looks good on you!"

My coat was the least of my worries. I was impatient to be out with all of you...A strange hope was raising its head in my heart.

We reached Anarkali...talking nineteen to the dozen! When we boarded the tonga, the tongawallah had asked one of us to come to the front to balance the weight. I was about to get down when Satbir had said—"Shabbo why don't you come?" Such a small thing, but that ache still lives in my heart...the weather of that precise moment is still imprinted on my mind, as also the place where the tonga had stopped so that you could change your seat. The noise and the brilliant lights of Anarkali had receded.... I don't remember who bought what...a book...Christmas card. And then we had gone to the Kashmiri tea vendor who sat in the shelter of a few shops to escape the sharp blasts of the cold winds. We had bought a bunch of narcissus flowers… their lovely perfume pervaded the atmosphere. I love narcissus… even now as then. No other flower has that lovely fragrance. Even today, whenever I see those flowers during winter, I always buy them, and that evening flashes before my mind's eye. Satbir had given me that bunch of flowers and we talked as we strolled…at what moment, at what point of time, Satbir took that bunch from me and gave it to you, I don't remember. But when those flowers left my hands for yours for a moment my heart stopped…perhaps tears had also come to my eyes…and they may have spilled over but then my heart saw sense…as if it had understood everything! I had glanced at you, you were very happy. It was not a mere bunch of flowers: he had given you something more. His love—true and pure. And I can still feel that love. At that time also I was not jealous of you…and I had not yet been able to gauge the anguish in my own heart.

Satbir's leave was over and his going away made our world desolate; we took out our books, dusted them and prepared to resume our studies. But we did not know that we would not sit for any more exams in Lahore. Tension was rising by the day. People were full of the talk of the change of government and the division of the country. And then all those things happened which one could not have imagined even in dreams. After the terrible riots in Pothohar, Lahore was no longer the Lahore it had been. A strange change had come over people…tension and anger simmered everywhere. Hatred filled every heart and your visits grew rare.

Then, one day, when I had just closed the door after Beji had gone to the gurudwara, there was a knock on the door.

"Jiti open the door, it is me, Satbir."

He stood at the door and as soon as I opened the door he asked—"Where is Beji?"

"She has just gone to the gurudwara. When did you come? What is it?" I was perturbed at his confusion.

"I came this morning. Dear Jiti please go and fetch Shabbo, fast!"

"To your place?"

"No, no, there are too many people there. I have something very important to do today… bring her over…quickly."

I could not refuse him. Your Ammi was also not at home, and I just said, "Come quickly, there is some important work," and you came with me. I was making some tea for the two of you as you talked in low voices. I had no idea what was being said, but when I entered the room Satbir had your hand in his and was saying—"What should we do? Come with me right away."

You wept silently as you twisted your *chunni* around your fingers. Satbir burst out, "Pakistan will be created…this is the truth. God knows what will happen, whether we can meet each other again or not…listen to me." But you kept on weeping and shaking you head, muttering "This is not possible, and you know it. What can I do?"

You both were very sad, and I was also under the shadow of your unhappiness. Surjit was upset. Suddenly, at that crossroads of our life our childhood vanished. Our innocence was submerged in tears. Could we not go back? Why did not Satbir tease me the way he always had? Why were we being told not to go out? I was upset at Satbir's unhappiness. How could I dispel it?

Those days also passed like a storm…our Lahore slipped through our hands. Some one gave an order and the riots started. We suffered greatly and couldn't reach each other…and then we got the news that you people were not at home. Surjit and I did go over once to check but the door had a big lock on it. Satbir also tried to find out about you…but then, we did not even know about ourselves. Everything changed with the coming of Pakistan…people were scattered and no one knew who went where, abandoning homes, lanes, neighbours… sometimes only with their bare lives…you too know all this, Shabbo.

And who knows where you are today? Wherever you are, I hope you are reading this letter, and know that we all still think of you. Satbir loved you deeply and went back repeatedly from time to time to look for you. Today, he is seated right here, before me. His son Jasbir, who is in the Indian Air Force, has been decorated for bravery in the Kargil war. Jasbir bears a striking resemblance to Satbir and looks like Satbir did those days.

"What have we come to! We used to love each other…and now we are killing each other…" Satbir talks about these things only with me.

"She said that we would be butchered if caught…I had begged her…and then she never met me…."

How things get stuck; time moves ahead and helplessly we seek to turn it back. But it is impossible to hold it.

How can I believe that you have forgotten him and me! Satbir's memory must still be entrenched in some corner of your heart… those *nargis* flowers which he had taken from me to hand over to you…do not let me sleep even today. I still dream that my beloved flowers were snatched away from me and I was left weeping. Tears spill over…but my lips smile. Satbir does not know anything. Perhaps he does not remember those flowers…he still thinks that I am young.

"I loved her Jiti…she was my first love…" he was saying.

"Yes I know," I answer. I could not bring myself to do anything at that time, and what could I do now?

Shabbo! You are indeed very lucky.

Translation: Tripti Jain

ONE'S OWN COUNTRY

Tahira Iqbal

Cowdung cakes had turned to ashes in the clay hearths embellished with minarets and round arches and decorative paintings. Clinging to the kitchen door, Daboo put up his snout in the air, and barked, clawing at the empty space as though it was teeming with cats. In his eagerness to understand the mystery, Daboo nudged Bashiran in the buttock. Their shaking heads seemed to acknowledge the existence of a mysterious presence.

"Now, she comes every day, and at the same time."

Faded pale eyes, sunk deep in the wrinkled folds suddenly shone with life.

"Nazir Ahmed! Do you not believe that she comes daily and at the same time?"

Specks of ash from the blackened chimney of the lantern floated in the air and up their nostrils. The smoking lantern cast weird shadows on the book. Badly caught between his quest for purpose and the realisation of his own inability, the boy was irritated. As he opened his mouth to answer, ash dust floated down his throat.

"Who can say when this ignorance will end!"

He flicked through his book, as though trying to urge on obstinate time to pass.

"What does your book say—that there are no spirits?"

The words from a toothless mouth trembled with some inner fear. The ashen cowdung cakes were still emitting smoke.

"Spirits exist, but the book does not say how they can be seen by dogs, and not by human beings!"

He rose in a huff as though he was the erudite teacher of a class of idiots, upsetting the *mudda*[1] he sat on and it rolled down the courtyard.

"But I can see everything! When she jumped into the well, right before my eyes, before her own mother's eyes...into the well!"

With each word her arms swung from right to left, and left to right.

"Your three maternal uncles were slaughtered with *kirpans*. Your father fell victim to bayonets, blood oozing from his eyes and mouth. Pappu had told her—'Nek begum, child, go bathe at the well.' And she jumped into the bottomless well to bathe. She never came out after her bath." Her fingers were moving in the air attesting the evidence.

"Nek Begum, child, go for a bath—oh daughter, go for a bath. The other girls have all come back.

"Oh, my daughter...oh mar jainwain dhiye...you jumped into the well...you had such lovely long hair...oh mar jaiwain dhiye... oh daughter, may you die. Your bright eyes brimmed with life...oh my daughter...

"Your slim long fingers reduced to nothing...

"Oh, my daughter go for a bath...!"

1 Mudda: A low stool made of cane and thick coir ropes

The shaking fingers gesticulated as though standing testimony to the tragic event. The acrid smoke from the embers filled the room with bitterness.

Drops of water from her nose dripped into the embers.

Picking up a fistful of kindling, Bashiran threw it on the smouldering ashes, and blew into the heap to light the fire. A black cloud of smoke rose from the heap and curled up the walls.

"Nek Begum, dhiye hai mar jaiwain dhiye..."

Suddenly, the silence was broken by the blast of a horn. Daboo matched the sound, bark by bark.

Nazir Ahmed opened the wooden gate. His three older brothers drove in on a tractor trolley.

The children rushed to the trolley to unload the carrots, radishes, cane and keanus. There was such a commotion in the trolley. The three stalwart young men retired to their rooms with their share of the goods. Their wives ladled out hot steaming food and took the covered trays into their rooms.

Bashiran picked up a roasted cob from the ash and dusting it with her hands, peeled it, grain by grain. Holding the corn in her palm she said—"Here, Bebe! You also eat some."

Bebe put a few corns into her toothless mouth. Her wrinkled face crumpled.

"Take it away, it is tasteless! Oh Bashiran bibi, what lovely corn we had in our own country! This corn!" She flung out her arm in disgust.

"What tasty corn Karnail Singh raised in his fields! Such big, full grains, we picked the best and filled our *chunni*s to take home. And then at home, Bebe would scold us...." Her laughter choked her.

"But this is from our own fields, what if it is tasteless." Nazir Ahmed fixed his gaze on the words on the page as though trying to discover something.

"Those lands were also like our own. He never stopped us, never said no. Fair complexion, black hair, saffron *kurta*. How handsome he looked! He was so dashing. He would draw cold water from the well! Cold and sweet water. Sweet like sherbet. Such a handsome man. He would say, 'Barkat bibi, why does water become so sweet in your pitcher?'

"The water of that well was sweet! But Karnail Singh...." The wind rushed into the room. "But Karnail Singh...he was so jovial."

"That's why he killed your whole Khawaish family."

The words hung in the air, as though trying to look for something.

"No, it was not Karnail Singh, who killed them. He was a very kind man! Very kind and gentle..."

"Then, it may have been Kaptan Singh who killed them. Or Laftain Singh. The killer was definitely a Singh!" Nazir Ahmed closed his book with a bang.

The wrinkled face gradually took on a serious look, as though busy with a difficult philosophical question and about to pronounce an important decision.

"Yes, Nazir Ahmed! But that Singh had no name. Some four days earlier Karnail Singh had gone to Amritsar, and on his return told your grandfather—'Chowdhary, there is some news. They say that the country is to be divided and the Muslims will have to go to Pakistan. But don't you worry, your house, cattle, livestock would all be properly looked after. It is a matter of only a few days. Then, things would be normal, and everyone will come back to their homes.' *Hai*! In the evening we locked the house as it was—full of things. Patted Bhuri."

The corncobs roasting in the ashes crackled. The smoke from the cowdung cakes choked their throats. Her mind reflected her anguish.

"Bebe, so what? Count the mercies of God and be thankful."

There was a tractor-trolley standing in one corner of the large compound. A thresher stood nearby.

A double storied solid house was overflowing with goods. The mangers were full of milch cows and about-to-calve buffaloes.

"Did you leave more than this behind?" The faces of the boys reflected the arrogance of their achievements and acquisitions.

"It was much less than this, but it had a different taste, Bashir Ahmed! That taste is found only in one's own country, Nasir Ahmed. What radishes we had back home! Such large radishes, and sweet as sugar!"

She could still taste the sweetness of that sugar in her mouth.

"The bitter of your own country is better than the sweet of another."

Irritated, Nazir Ahmed again opened his book. The pages kept fluttering in the wind.

"Don't call it another country, Nazir Ahmed. Don't say that. Your three uncles, young and strong, lie there in pieces. Your grandfather's blood has been spilt on that earth. Two of your father's brothers were lost there. Who knows they may have gone back there, to their homes? They were not all that young. One was eight and the other ten. They understood things, they knew the way home. Doesn't your book have Karnail Singh's address?"

"*Arrey*, Bebe! Who knows which *kirpan* may have butchered them, poor things. They wouldn't be with Karnail Singh..."

"Yes, what you say may also be right."

"Hai! Nek Begum! Your father told you to bathe in the well. You didn't come out after your bath.

"Nek Begum, *dhiye ni, tunwi nahawin nun ja.*
Ai mar jaiwain dhiye ne."
(Nek Begum, daughter, you also go for a bath! Hai, girl may you die.)

"Bashiran, *arrey o* Bashiran, open the door," a powerful voice trampled the grief underfoot.

"Look, here comes the witch. The black witch threw away her own heart! Bashiran was barely six months old, when she threw her on a heap of corpses with dogs and vultures feasting on them. She threw her away. Had I not been coming behind her…"

"Had you not been coming behind, how would she have become your daughter-in-law? I had said it there and then that whosoever has saved her may look after her, keep her or kill her."

Breathing hard through her mouth and nose, Fajju tottered in and sat down near the hearth. The numerous untold stories shone in the wrinkles of her face.

Wrapped in a blue striped shawl, the pipe of a hookah clenched in his mouth, an old man came into the room.

"Faqir Mohammad! Tell him that Karnail Singh did not kill us. Not even Jarnail Singh. We were…we were…"

Before Faqir Mohammad could say anything, she herself began relating the truth.

"Karnail Singh was a very good man. He had presented me with a red suit. He said—'Barkat bibi don't take it to be an ordinary suit. Someone has woven his affection into its warp and woof.' That was enough to set a sixteen-year-old's heart aflutter."

"He was full of fun and humour."

"Listen to this! He was full of humour!" Baba Dinu had a fit of cough and spat out a blob of phlegm into the air. Dabboo joined him bark by bark.

"....Khari inha di mat
hus hus landiyan yaariyan
ro ro daindiyan das..."

(They are so wise/they enchant you with their love/and weep as they retract.)

"We had thought something else all along! Karnail Singh a good man!"

"Listen to this old man. What did you think? Was I not aware of what you were upto! You followed Surender Kaur about like a dog. She was my sister, we had exchanged dupattas. She would tell me everything."

She covered her face with her dupatta. As though she had gathered the distant time in its fold.

"There was no other woman like Surender Kaur in the whole of Punjab. Her long black plait swung like a snake. Colourful salwars! Tall and erect, she'd find it difficult to go through a door straight. She would take out the folded roti from the colourful basket and I would snatch the roti. The pat of butter would melt on the roti. She would turn back and look at me...she was coming with me to Pakistan... she said. 'What is there in a country! Your country is mine, don't take it as another country...'"

The interesting story had lessened the seriousness of the quarrel. Throats were choked with tears. The young tried to dispel the tension that had built up. They were well acquainted with these tense moments.

"Here, take an orange, they are from our own orchards." Nasir Ahmed pulled a sackful of oranges and emptied it.

"Sister Barkat! What oranges we had in our country, large and juicy. Sweet as honey!" A new sentiment had been articulated.

"These radishes and carrots, raw sugar, and trees of small mangoes. Rows and rows of small trees in Karnail Singh's fields, as though young women wrapped in green dupattas, with their tinkling anklets walking in a row...." Suppressed laughter could be heard.

"We would collect the mangoes in our orange *chunnis*."

Memories shone in their eyes like stars, congested their hearts. Eighty-year-old women went exploring the dark ruins of their memories, illuminating everything with a golden hue.

"Were mangoes grown only on Karnail Singh's land? They were grown elsewhere also, and they were also very sweet." Baba Dinu was upset with the intensity of the emotions.

"They were found elsewhere also, but the ones grown in your fields were always sour. Your abba laboured hard, but they were sour. Karnail Singh's mangoes were very sweet."

Another memory was dredged up from the well of memories, bubbles rising to the top.

"He would say give me some, and I would throw a mango at him and it would get entangled in his hair. Here eat some...another one...and I would hide in a cool corner in the orchard."

"Nazir Ahmed, you have studied two classes?"

Nazir Ahmed got up in a huff as though his certificates had been set on fire right before his eyes.

"Bebe, I have told you time and again that I am taking my XII class exam."

"*Achcha...achcha*, twelve classes, Karnail Singh had passed four classes." The response was weightier.

'Then, he was illiterate," he said and began throwing stones at the dogs lurking in the groves of trees.

"No, Nazir Ahmed, don't say that. He was a well read man."

"He was well-read, that is why he cut down all of them with his *kirpan* and pushed Nek Begum into the well!"

"He did not throw her into the well, no, he did not push her into the well. Her father told her—'Nek Begum go, bathe in the well.' She went to bathe, and then did not come back."

Hiding in the groves of neem and peepal trees, Dabboo was barking at the wind, and clawing the ground, as though cats were lurking all over.

"Nek Begum, daughter, you also go and bathe, hai mar jawain dhiye ni, nahawan nun ja, hor te dhiyan naha ke ghar aiyain, hor te dhiyan naha ghar aiyan hai mar jaiwan...."

(Oh, daughter, may you die, go and bathe, daughters of others have come back after bathing, oh may you die....)

The day the village got electricity, Nazir Ahmad had sat for his first exam paper, and the next day he had to sit for Pakistan Affairs paper. He sat till late in the night studying for his exam.

Rays of the morning sun crept into the room on the terrace, glittering on the crockery and steel utensils arranged on the racks above and on the brocade quilt of Bebe sleeping in the room there. Only her face could be seen from under that orange quilt. As though it had been soaked in saffron by the golden light of the sun. The butterflies floating around shone in the gold of the rising sun.

Bebe put a pinch of snuff in her mouth and her shrunken cheeks began working on it.

"Nazir Ahmed, has the village been electrified?"

"Yes, Bebe, it has, finally." Sounds of snores could be heard from the various cots, spread around.

"Dabboo is quiet, Nazir Ahmed the sun has come out...Now, how ... will he not bark now?"

"Yes, why should he bark?"

"Is the print of your book clearer now? Tell me, Nazir Ahmed."

"Yes, it is."

"Have you not been able to find Karnail Singh's address?"

"Bebe!" The boy was irritated by this. The question seemed to hammer him. The silence outside was lightened by the increasing brightness. Dabboo could neither be heard nor seen. He seemed to have disappeared somewhere in the thick groves of neem and peepal trees.

"Nazir Ahmed, I have to tell you something."

"What is it, Bebe?" The hammer seemed to become heavier.

"Nazir Ahmed, write it in your book. Write it down. Write that Karnail Singh did not kill us. The killer was some Singh." The hammer blows were incessant. "Yes, but he had no name. All four brothers were slaughtered. My husband was cut to pieces. My sons were lost there. Nek Begum..."

"Bebe!" Nazir Ahmed sprang up in agitation.

"The village told her go to the well and bathe. She went to bathe." She went on like a cassette tape which does not know how to stop on its own.

"She bathed, and did not come out."

"Nek Begum, dhiye ni tunvi nahawan ja, hai mar jaiwain dhiye ni hai mar jaiwain, dhiya ni mari oh doongri chaal."

(Nek Begum, daughter, you also go for a bath, oh, my daughter may you die, may you die, daughter mine, oh daughter you took a very deep jump.)

"Hai mar jawan...mar jaiwain...hai..."

The mournful refrain spread in the whole house filling it with tumultuous grief.

Translation: Tripti Jain

THE OINTMENT

Sanwal Dhami

Till 1947 Nauru Nangal was a centre of trade between the people of the plains and the folks from the mountains. Those days, the aroma of tobacco from Peshawar and spices from the far off mountains would rise into the air from the bazaar of this village, wafting all around. Nestling at the foothills of the Shivalik mountains, and half hidden behind the ancient peepal, mango and black plum trees, this village had been settled by Rajput Muslims of the Nauru caste.

The Rajputs, who owned the lands, lived in large havelis and spent their time smoking hukkas and gossiping. Lands would be leased out to Hindu *Sainis** or Sikh *Labanas*[1]*.These peasants, along with other crops, also grew tobacco for their landlords.

Mian Mohammad Baksh was the most prominent person in the village. People called him Mianji out of respect. When he moved around the village in his high-crowned turban, salwar kameez, and

---

1 *Castes involved in agriculture and weaving.

gold-embroidered *jootis*, people would stand up to greet him. He was often seen on horseback, a gun slung over his shoulder. People would bow and greet him with salaams and muttering a reply, he would move ahead. On such occasions, the trot of his mare would become little sharper, and his neck a little more stiff.

He was the Chowdhary of the village. The largest haveli in the village was his; it was in the eastern part of the village, standing on half an acre of land. He owned most of the land—full eighty acres. He was the owner of five wells. Four of these wells were on his lands. The fifth one was in the haveli. The western corner of the wall of the haveli divided the parapet of the well into two: half of the well was in the courtyard, and, the other half in the lane. It was from this well that the other Rajputs drew water. There were separate, and small wells, for non-Muslims and Muslim menials of the village.

Both Mian's begum and his daughter Nafeesa, wore a burqa whenever they stepped out. Nafeesa had very few friends. Few persons were permitted to cross the threshold of the haveli.

Fazala, of the hakims visited the haveli almost every day, to shave Mian. One morning, Fazala suddenly looked up and saw a beautiful face smiling at him. There was something in Nafeesa's eyes, but, he was neither of the age nor of the status to be able to give a name to this 'something'.

It was a matter of common knowledge that Mian's daughter Nafeesa was very beautiful, but it was Fazal alone who had seen her beauty with his own eyes. He eagerly related this event to his friend Karmu Saini.

"Karmu, she is even more intoxicating than poppy flowers!"

When this comment, repeated by Karma, travelling by lips, traversed the village, and crossed the threshold of Mian's haveli, the house was shaken by an earthquake. To Mian, everything seemed to tremble and shake.

Aslam, the cobbler, was immediately dispatched to Karamdin's home. Karamdin was Fazal's father. He had a barber's shop, and also practised *hikamat*—the indigenous system of medicine. His home was behind the shop. The son tended the shop, as the father went to neighbouring villages to dispense medicines, and to pursue the duties of a barber. The family was known for an ointment which could heal the oldest and deepest wound. Karamdin was a pious man and the village and its surroundings treated him with great respect. But, going to Mian's haveli, that day, he felt that the stains of infamy on his turban were deepening with every step. Fazala walked behind his Abba, with a frightened heart and faltering steps.

The sound of the slap had echoed in the whole haveli. It had seemed to Fazala that Nafeesa was watching the whole tamasha standing at the window, and the well had also laughed and applauded! After this incident, the doors of the haveli were closed to the hakim's family. Fazala, shamed and dejected, went about in stoic silence.

But, now six months later, this humiliation was to turn into respect. The wound in Mian's foot had turned septic. First, he had gone to some famous hakim for treatment. Then, as the wound worsened, he had thought of Karamdin. Fazala experienced a thrill of triumph when he had turned away the servant from the haveli, who had arrived with Mian's message. He had felt that Mian's three-storeyed haveli was yearning to shrink and be put away in a small box of ointment. He went about telling one and all about it till the evening. At sunset, when Abba came home, he was extremely annoyed when he heard the whole story.

"You have ruined all—everything our generations had earned, Fazala! Oye, never be arrogant about this ointment. Else, all the healing power that we have been blessed with, will vanish. Never discriminate between friend and foe, only look at the wound, son."

Without eating anything, he had picked up his medicine bag and had rushed to the haveli. A small box of ointment had become a bridge between two families that had been cut off from each other.

Celebrating fairs, festivals and gurupurabs, the village was ambling along, like Shamshu's ox going round the oil press. But this march of shared happiness was jolted by a piece of news: the division of the country. Fear and uncertainty had begun obstructing the activities of this village. Life was moving away from the *chaupals* and fields, lanes, religious centres, shops and forges, and slowly shrinking within the walls of homes. The information being relayed by Mian's radio was confirmed by incidents in the area. A fine line had been drawn in the hearts of the villagers, and it was getting stronger and clearer with each passing day.

Like his father, Satta, the ironsmith, was famous in the whole region for his battleaxes and scythes. The Jats of the neighbouring village, Lahli Khurd, had sent for him. He did not return for many days. People had now started imagining all sorts of things. The doubts in the minds of the Muslims were growing.

When Satta did come home after five days, he was barefoot and bareheaded, and groaning with pain. Exhausted and broken. His eyes were red due to lack of sleep, as though dripping blood. His right hand was wrapped in his own blood-soaked turban. While sharpening a battleaxe the boy using the sledge hammer, tired and sleepy, had hit the hammer on his hand, utterly crushing two middle fingers.

When he told his mother about getting hurt while sharpening the wedge of a plough, she had retorted angrily—"Don't try to hide things from me! I gave birth to you. The Jats have taken up battleaxes in place of ploughs, what ploughs are you talking about? The Jats took you. Even God is afraid of these bastards. We are menials and workers, we cannot play favourites."

Satta had listened to this tirade head bowed.

The evening Satta had returned, a meeting of the Muslims took place at Mian's haveli. The 'untouchable' and 'low' class of yesterday now appeared to be co-religionists to the Rajput Muslims. After seating the oil men, cobblers, barbers and drumbeaters near them, ways and means of safety were being discussed.

"Chowdharys", Chiragdin *mirasi*[2] had said with folded hands, "You were our masters earlier, and even now you are our masters. We poor people are wholly under your protection. Masters, whatever you say would be our command."

After a long discussion, Mian stood up. There was great sadness in his voice and today his head was slightly bowed.

"The first thing is..." he had seemed a stranger and dejected to all, as he stood there with folded hands—"We shouldn't trust either the Hindus or the Sikhs! Second, always be prepared for a fight. If you have no weapons, at least collect stones and bricks. Third, women must not step out of their homes at all, and for a few days, even men should not leave the village. The fourth thing is that we must establish contact with our co-religionists of the neighbouring villages and discuss plans for joint action. We must take all precautions to protect ourselves, especially the well. About leaving the village..." at this juncture his voice grew hoarse with emotion.

"We'll decide in a few days after keeping a close watch on the situation."

This last sentence had made everyone emotional. Unable to speak they could not voice their approval of Mian's instructions; they only nodded to show their agreement and rose to leave, when

---

2 A caste of bards and entertainers

they heard Satta's mother's wailing—"O hakim, come quickly! Satta is badly hurt." For a minute the assembly, about to break up, was rendered speechless.

"Listen, hakim..." Noor Mohammad had said after a few moments, turning to Karamdin. "If you want to live with your own community, then don't give any medicine to the ironsmith."

"He has just returned from Lahli after sharpening their battle-axes...mother-fucker..." Hasan declared venomously.

"Let him die a dog's death," Hasan declared venomously.

Standing at the threshold, holding the door jamb for support, and hearing all this, Satta's mother had been deeply troubled. She had returned home with tired dragging steps.

On his way home, Karamdin tried to imagine Satta sharpening battleaxes. But, each time he could only hear him groaning with pain.

Satta was of the same age as Fazala, and had been his schoolmate. Satta's father, Meena, who had died last year, was a close friend of Karamdin. Karamdin picked up his medicine bag from the shop avoiding others and afraid of being seen, had gone to Satta's home with trembling hands.

"If your religion has awakened, then the other also will not go against his own people! The hakim will not come. Now, you can call out to the Jats of Lahli, who couldn't even find a piece of cloth to bind your wounds. What a mighty saviour of faith!"

When Karamdin came through the front door, Satta's mother was surprised, and silenced. Satta also stopped groaning, and bowed his head. He did not look up even when the ointment was applied and the wounds properly bandaged. Swallowing his pain, he remained silent.

By morning, Satta's wounds had stopped bleeding, but bloody news streamed into the village from all over the country. Riots and killings had broken out in the surrounding villages. News of Pathans of Bassi Ali Khan, Bassi Hasat Khan, Bassi Daud Khan, Bassi Kalan and Bassi Jaura leaving their twenty-two villages had filled the hearts and minds of the Rajputs of Nauru Nangal with fear.

On the third day, in the scorching afternoon heat, a group of very young Sikhs, battleaxes in their hands, had reached the bazaar of Nauru Nangal. Terrified people had bolted their doors watching the lane through the windows with dread in their hearts. The group had stopped in front of the hakim's shop. A Sikh, no more than a boy, stepped forward to knock at the door, but there had been no answer from within...

"Oye, Fazala, this is Dhanna. Please open the door." A Sardar of medium height with light eyes, called out with familiarity.

Fazala opened the door and about eight or ten Sikh boys walked into the shop.

"What do you want, sons?" Karamdin had asked a little timidly.

"Bapu has been badly hurt, chacha. Pick up your medicine bag and hurry up. The boys would escort you back." The hakim was a little thoughtful at what the light-eyed boy had just said.

This was Dhanna, from the neighbouring village Lahli Khurd. Dhanna was Fazal's classmate, and friend. They had often skipped classes together to go to fairs. Many a time they had been soundly thrashed by Master Fateh Mohammad and Pandit Dina Nath. Both had dropped out of school after failing their ninth class. Twenty-two, Dhanna was now decked out as a grown up turbaned Sardar. He had collected a band of boys from the area and formed a group. He was himself the jathedar-leader. Jathedar Dhanna Singh Bains! These boys attacked villages, looted houses, murdered Muslims, and abducted beautiful girls and women. They would use them for a few days themselves, and then pass them on to others. If they found someone in need of a woman, they would also earn some money out of them.

"That may be, but, son…" the hakim roused himself from deep thought. "Mian has forbidden us to leave the village."

"Chacha!" Dhanna had said angrily—"What are you talking about? Mian is nothing today. Let me tell you, it is we who control the whole area now. We have driven out the Musalmans from twenty villages around here, chacha! This Nauru Nangal village has been spared because of *you*. You come with me without a word. We will overselves settle it with Mian.' There was real menace in Dhanna's voice.

"Abba, go, Taya would be in great pain," Fazal was really concerned.

"That is right son, but…" Karamdin went no further, but was thinking about the situation.

"But what, Abba? You yourself say that the ointment…"

Before Fazala could finish, Karamdin had picked up his medicine bag.

Coming out into the lane, he began walking before the group. As soon as they were out of the village, the boys quickened their pace. They neither talked to one another, nor did they say anything to Karamdin.

This silence deepened Karamdin's doubts and fears all the more.

When the boys suddenly took the road to the *takiya* – a Muslim monastery – Karamdin was greatly upset. But, the very next moment he saw the horses tethered to the trees in front of the *takiya*. In his heart he prostrated without bowing his head, and prayed for his safety.

"Look, Chacha, we are very close to each other…I cannot lie to you anymore. Bapu is not injured. We have brought you here because we respect you," Dhanna Singh said moving closer to him.

At this, Karamdin had placed the bag on the ground with shaking hands.

"You have access to every home, hakim. Tell us how much ammunition there is in Nauru Nangal! Which Rajput has a gun?' This was another boy.

To Karamdin, the *takiya* seemed to be shaking. He sat down hastily on the parapet.

"We are poor people, working with scissors and razors, son. What do we know about guns?" His voice trembled.

"Don't do this Chacha. Please think of me at least. If these hot-headed ones lose their heads, then I won't be able to control them...." With this request, Dhanna Singh sat down beside a dejected Karamdin.

"Look uncle, you'll go to your Pakistan. I am like Fazala. If nothing else, you can give me the prescription of the ointment." Dhanna said in a soft tone dripping sarcasm. The boys had laughed. But, Karamdin's whole body was seized by a cold fury. He had answered fearlessly—"Oye, Dhania, how would you understand the sanctity of this ointment? One needs the mind and compassion of Bhai Kanhaiyaji to be able to inherit the prescription."

The boys were surprised at the change in Karamdin's behaviour.

One of them took two steps forward and aimed his axe at Karamdin's head. The hakim was taken aback.

"O no. Zaila! He is our chacha!" Dhanna had warned, and Zaila retreated.

Dhanna moved closer to the hakim and said—"Come Chacha, tell me which Rajput has the most beautiful daughter?"

The hakim was shaking with rage. Standing up and gesticulating to express his anger, he said, "You should be ashamed of yourself, son, they are all my daughters! Daughters are daughters, not beautiful or ugly." With this he fell silent.

"*Oye* Sardara," the boy with moustaches drawn to points was now visibly annoyed. "We did tell you that we should pick up some Rajput. Now, you get the information from your chacha. You were so proud of him! We know these menials well.They are very obstinate. Now, get your chacha to give you the information about the guns!"

"And also the prescription of the ointment..." the boy in the black kurta laughed.

"Tell me, are you going to practice medicine and give up farming with that prescription?" The boy with earrings had laughed.

"You are just wasting your time." This was the dark one who said this regretfully.

When all the other boys agreed with what the one with moustaches had said, Dhanna stood up.

"Do whatever you want." With this, he unhitched his horse, and jumping on to the saddle, galloped away. Karamdin was struggling to find words to stop him, but, Dhanna had disappeared from sight.

The boy who had remained silent all along, suddenly raised his axe with both hands and struck Karamdin on the chest. He screamed and collapsed. The boy with moustaches had struck Karmdin six or seven blows on his shoulders. Then, the boys rode off, in the direction their leader had taken.

When Karamdin did not return home by the evening, his family was really worried. Despite his mother's and sisters' attempts to stop him, Fazala, with Gulzar of the *bharai*s[3] had gone towards Lahli. Their hearts were trembling with the fear that something untoward had

3 The drum beaters' caste

happened. Even the slightest sound was enough to frighten them. As they passed the *takiya*, they heard someone groaning. Some one was saying "*Hai Allah*" in a very weak voice, intermittently. For one moment, Fazal was nonplussed. He seemed to be rooted to the ground. He stood there, motionless, like a statue.

Gulzar shook him, and he recovered. Crying, he ran towards the monastery.

"*Hai o Rabba*!" He was crying bitterly as he gathered his father in his arms.

"Be sensible, Fazal, get aside and let's take *taya* home," Gulzar picked up the hakim's shattered body and carried it on his shoulder. They walked with rapid steps towards the village. Clutching at his abba's dangling arms, Fazal walked behind Gulzar. Karamdin's groans had stopped. Fazal kept on crying—"Abba, say something", "Abba speak", all the way. On reaching home, Karamdin was lowered on to a cot, but, by then he was dead. He had bled profusely lying in the *takiya*, and also on the sandy path leading towards Lahli.

Hearing the crying and wailing the whole village had collected around them. The hearts of the Muslims were trembling with fear. The heat of religious violence was knocking at the doors of Nauru Nangal.

"This is the result of betraying the community. He sneaked off to treat the wounds of the kafirs." Some one from the crowd standing outside Fazal's shop said, and the other expressed their agreement.

At Karamdin's burial, Satta also stood in a corner, wiping his tears with the corner of his turban.

When Karmu said, "There are very deep wounds inflicted by an axe on the hack," Satta's head had drooped.

As they returned from the cemetery, poison seemed to have infected the atmosphere of the village. Everyone was full of fear and apprehension. There was anger and bitterness in the hearts of the Muslims. By the evening, a rumour had spread that they had made plans to massacre the Hindus and Sikhs, who were in a minority. The Hindus and Sikhs had collected all their valuables and had loaded their carts. Locking their houses, they had set off on the roads to the neighbouring villages.

"Brothers, we were here because we have faith in you. But you are leaving us to be humiliated and massacred. Don't do this to us." Karmu's eyes had spilled over at this appeal from Fazala. He could not say anything even though he wanted to. He turned away his face and prodded the bullocks to move. Sad and dejected, Fazal had watched him till he turned the corner of the lane, and disappeared from sight.

That evening, the last meeting was held at Mian's haveli.

"Just pack your valuables. There should be no delay whatsoever, this village is now no longer ours; this country is not ours. There is nothing more precious than honour and respect. Kill your daughters and sisters, but let them not fall into the hands of kafirs to be humiliated. As soon as you hear the watchman call, assemble at the masjid!" Mian's words had dried in his throat.

People were bundling up their goods with tears in their eyes. Soon, the watchman would call, signalling their departure. They waited tearfully, their hearts full of fear. Then, suddenly the sound of drums was heard. Shouts of "*Bole So Nihal*" rent the skies. After some shouting and ranting, *"Allah O Akbar"* could be heard from the havelis of the Rajputs. Sounds of gun shots and clashing of swords and axes also filled the air for some time. But, gradually, the attackers gained ground. Screams rose from one house and then another.

The two wells – of the pandits and Mian's – were full of corpses. Many Rajputs themselves cut their daughters' throats. Mian had been shot dead and his begum had jumped into the well. Nafeesa had hidden herself behind a pile of mattresses. In the midst of this uproar, Minder of the Chambawalia had climbed to the top floor. He found Nafeesa and taking the stunned and pleading Nafeesa forcibly into his arms, rushed down the stairs. Putting her on his horse, he clattered away into the darkness.

"Dog! Sister's…," Dhanna had shouted after him in fury.

"He has betrayed the Gurus! Follow the traitor!"

Many boys had set their horses in pursuit of Minder after this order from the *jathedar*. But they came back empty-handed.

The village was steeped in mourning and sorrow.

Many homes were spattered with blood. The wounded were suffering silently. Living bodies were shedding tears over the dead bodies scattered all over, as though, screams and wails had been banned. Some were so scared that they were still hiding.

Close to midnight, a voice full of sorrow and pleading had shaken the frightened and sorrowing people.

"Rise brothers, wake up. This is not the time to mourn. I am Satta, of the ironsmiths. I have run all the way from Lahli. There is to be an attack on the village at dawn. They have taken the final decision. Get up, and leave now to take shelter in the camp at Chak Saadu!"

Nobody believed a single word of what the Sikh was telling them. To most it seemed to be a trick by Dhanna's gang.

"*Oiye* Fazalia, my brother, if you are alive, please wake up. Explain to these people. Those sinners are going to kill everyone before the night is out. In the name of uncle Karamdin. *Oiye*, trust me! At least open the door!" Satta's strong voice had shrunk to a thin child-like wail.

When Fazal got up, his mother and sisters pleaded with him not to open the door.

"Have we already not suffered by the betrayal of these Sikhras?"

"I beg you not to open the door! If nothing else, think of your sisters," his mother had cried.

But Fazal had opened the door and come out into the lane.

He and Satta had run about the lanes, calling out to people.

When they heard Fazal's voice, the scared and stunned people stirred into life getting up from their watch near the dead bodies of their beloved ones. After kissing their lifeless faces, after apologising for leaving them without coffins and unburied, they collected their scattered bundles with trembling hands and walked out; bidding farewell to their homes, kissing their doorjambs, shedding tears on their thresholds. With tired steps they came out into the lanes and collected near the masjid. Their throats choked with tears, they embraced one another wordlessly. The heads of powerful Rajputs were now resting on the shoulders of cobblers and drum-beaters. As though the sorrowing hearts had completely forgotten all the lessons of caste distinctions!

The caravan of suffering people had set out behind Satta and Fazal towards an unwanted, unasked for, and unseen land.

They reached Chak Saadu camp before sunrise where a Baluch regiment was posted for their protection.

On his way back to the village, Satta had felt as though he was going to a graveyard. He had himself sent off the soul of the village far away, towards a distant destination.

Dhanna's gang was looting the ruined village.

"Who informed these Mussalas? If I get hold of the traitor, I swear by the Guru. I'll kill him like a dog!" The Singhs were furious.

Meherdin Nambardar's house was full of dead bodies. His young daughter lay near the kitchen with a sword passed through her breast.

"O you bastards! What have you done! You should at least look at the face before you attack!" Dhanna had turned the dead face with soft hands; for a moment his eyes flickered over her breasts.

By sunrise, the Jats had loaded their carts with the loot and departed for their villages. Their faces shone with happiness and excitement.

"Which village are we invited to tonight?" Jagata of Bathula had asked Santa.

"Bhullial Ratha is the only one left. There are many wealthy parties in that village. Then, there is an invitation from Dhanna tonight," Santa had said.

"How is that, Santiya?" Jagata had enquired.

"Minder has taken Mian's butterfly. The elder Rath has three daughters. Each more beautiful than the other! Dhanna has picked the best-looking of them to install in his home!" Santa summed up the situation with a laugh.

The Hindus and Sikhs who had left Nauru Nangal, came back the next day. Satta had taken the lead in burying the dead. Mian's burial had been the most difficult.

"How elegant and proud he was! The property he owned and the respect he commanded! All gone in a moment! Is this what life is all about?" Satta could not stop his tears, some of which fell on Mian's chest as the body lay in the grave.

The mad winds of violence had slowly abated. The storms darkening the skies had, also finally settled down.

The Jats who had taken the lead in rioting and looting, now took the lead in grabbing the lands. The loot they had filled their homes with was a matter of great satisfaction.

But the ones who were to get the lands of the Rajputs in Nauru Nangal had also arrived: Bhinders. Klers and Bajwas from Sialkot. There were also some Brahmins with them, but as good and skillful in cultivation of land as the Jats. The daughters of these 'newcomers' would not let the boys of the Sainis and Lubanas even cough.

The language that these newcomers spoke, their clothes and their behaviour, all seemed strange and alien to the old inhabitants of the area.

"The ones who have gone were much better," someone would comment sadly.

"You are right! They were much, much better." Everyone would agree.

"These damn riots snatched the best from us," another would add.

"And left us with these rascals," someone else would say with great bitterness, and all present would nod their heads in agreement.

The ones from Sialkot had turned the masjid into a gurudwara by ceremonially installing the Guru Granth Sahib there. There was already a gurudwara of the Lubanas, and the carpenters. This new gurudwara was still called the 'Masjidwala Gurudwara'. It was not very easy to wipe out the names and marks of those who had gone away. Neither could anyone stop talking about them, nor could their faces be obliterated from their minds.

Santa Singh had insisted, time and again, that Mian's fields should now be called *his* lands. Kaura Mal Jhangi also had the same complaint that his home was still known as Dilshad's *chaubara*. Likewise, even after four decades, Sher Mohammad's haveli was still not known by Chaman Singh Bajwa's name. The neem tree standing in Hans brahmin's courtyard was still 'Hasandin's neem'.

"Forty years have passed under its shade, yet it is still not ours," Hansa brahmin's son would say with a sad heart. In the same way, Mian's kothi and hakim's shop were still the same for everyone.

This is a recent event.

Summer had just begun.

The mango trees of Nauru Nangal had just started blooming.

A stranger, rather different looking from the local inhabitants,, got down from the minibus at the bus stop. He carried a suitcase. Tall and lean with a trimmed beard, he was wearing a salwar kameez, and a white turban on his head. As he entered the village bazaar, people looked at him rather keenly.

He had also stared at things around with great care, and then stopped in front of a shop. Taking him to be a customer, the shop attendant called out to him. He came into the shop with a sad look on his face.

The same wooden door, the same walls, and the same skylight... but the people were different! His eyes filled with tears.

"What do you want, sir?"

He wanted his own village back, forever; his own Nauru Nangal.

"What may I show you?" The boy had asked again, putting his hand on a roll of material.

He wanted to see all those faces who had been so dear that it had been impossible for him to pass a day without looking upon them.

The boy again said—"Do buy something, it is your own shop".

His heart filled with great sadness. He came out of the shop, and walked on towards Satta's home with rapid steps.

"God willing, he should be healthy and alive." With each step his heartbeat quickened.

In place of Satta's forge there stood a flourmill. An oldish man was lying on a bare cot, under the shade of the mulberry tree, lost in deep thought. The stranger had stopped near the cot and stood there, trying to recognise him.

"Satta!" He said bending slightly on the cot.

"Who is it?" Satta sat up and peered through his thick glasses.

"Oh! Have you forgotten me so soon? You yourself sent me away!"

"*Balle bai balle*! O Fazal, you!"

"This is great, yaar! I had given up all hope!" He sprang up and eagerly embraced Fazal. They stood silent for some time, tears rolling down their cheeks. Then, they pulled apart as a small crowd gathered around them. Children had already begun shouting in the lanes.

"Someone wearing salwar kameez has come to the miller's!"

"A Muslim has come to the village!"

"A Pakistani has come to the ironsmith's!"

A small crowd jostled around the mill till late at night. People would come in, and then leave. They enquired about his welfare, told him about themselves, and extended invitations to Fazala to visit their homes.

"Don't worry, brothers. I am here for the next five-seven days. We shall meet daily. We will talk daily. This *is* my village, my own. I will surely visit all of you!" Fazal gave the same answer to each one of them.

Satta and Fazal sat talking late into the night. Fazal had narrated the whole story to him, the story of pain, poverty and sorrow, the naked dance of death during the journey from Camp Saadu to Lahore, the story of beginning a new life in a strange land, strange place and amidst strange people. His throat choked many a time in the telling. Time and again he wiped his eyes.

Then, after a long silence, he spoke with some pride– 'Satta, now I have a shop in the best bazaar in Lahore. Both my sons are looking after it. My daughter is happy in her own home. I have a little money also. By God's grace life is very comfortable.'

"Don't you practice your hakimi these days?" Satta had asked.

"Sometimes I still make the ointment. People come from long distance with their wounds... yes... I have brought some boxes for the villagers also..." With this, Fazal had given a slight laugh, but Satta's eyes were filled with tears.

"How long will they last?" He had thought with a sad heart. Hearts are full of wounds. First, the attack on the guru's *dwara*, then, the massacre in Delhi, killing of innocent Hindus. What does Fazal know about these? He may go on preparing the ointment till he is worn out. Who keeps an account of hearts? How does he know how deep the wounds of Punjab are? Why Punjab alone? The whole country, and even the world, is in the same condition.

Next morning, Fazal had gone out even before the sun had risen fully. Today, he was a guest in every home.

People welcomed him by pouring oil at the threshold before he entered, the customary welcome for brides and honoured guests. Fresh sheets would be spread on the cots. Men would gather around to spend time with him, abandoning even their most important tasks. For women and children, he was a different being. The best of food would be placed before him. While all this honour and love were being showered on him, the memory of that ugly night haunted Fazal, when he had to flee his beloved village to save his life.

"The tricks that life plays!" And with this thought tears would spring to his eyes.

"Forgive us, Fazal! There were other compulsions at that time. I couldn't say anything to you the last time. I can never forget that last time. I could see you standing near the cart." With this Karma Saini had had burst into tears like a child.

"After how many days did you return to the village then?" Fazal had tried to change the direction of the conversation into another channel.

"The next day," Karma had answered immediately.

"See Karma, we have lived forty years after that, But how? That only I know, or my God!" Fazal choked on his words.

At night, when both Satta and Fazala were stretched out on cots, Fazala had asked—"Satta what was the thing that had made enemies of friends who meant more than ones own life?"

"You can call it stupidity. Many factors combine, and man loses his reason," Satta had said after thinking over the question for some time.

"You tell me about yourself. Why did you go to Lahli that day to sharpen scythes and axes?"

Satta was shaken to the core of his soul. He had not expected such a question about the time long past from Fazal.

He tried to recollect the scattered details of that time for some moments. Then, with a slight cough, he said—"They had taken me on some other pretext. I had been moved by the stories of atrocities on the gurus by the Muslims. You can say I was blinded at that time." He had said this with great sadness, and had waited for some support from Fazal. But Fazal said nothing.

"Then, when I was wounded, the leaders of the community could not find even a strip of a cloth for me. They took my turban and wound it round my arm, and sent me off! Blood kept dripping the whole way. I was in terrible pain…" Satta was silent for quite some time.

Fazal still did not think it appropriate to make an answer.

"…Then, when chacha Karamdin came to attend to my injuries, hiding from his own community, I had thought of Bhai Kanhaiyaji. Chacha had seemed to be a true Singh of the gurus. If Sikhs like Dhanna Singh are weighed against Chacha, then, by god, they would be lighter! Very much lighter!" Suddenly, Satta's voice had thickened.

Fazala had then thought of Abba, who lay buried in some grave nearby. He was filled with a feeling of pride.

Next morning, as soon as they had got up, Fazal had asked Satta—"Was Mian's whole family killed?"

"No!" This brief answer made Fazal's old body tremble.

"Poor Mian and Begum were killed, but…but Nafeesa is still alive. She is in Chambewal…the wife of a Jat."

Fazal's heart was filled with great sadness at this. "Really?" He said with a sigh. "Satta, I want to meet Nafeesa."

Satta immediately called his son Amolak Singh, a science teacher in a village school near Chambewal.

"Kaka, listen carefully. You have to go to Chambewal. Go to the western side of the village, near the house of Sardar Chowdhary, which is near the well of the pandits. Towards the right of these two go to the house with the lilac tree. This is the house of Minder Singh Jat. Nafeesa is his wife. She is a daughter of this village. Actually, she must be having some other name now. Tell her that Fazala of the hakims has come from Pakistan. He wants to meet her. Bring her on your cycle, if she agrees.'

As Satta was explaining to his son, Fazal sat with his eyes closed to go back into his own past.

A beautiful face peeping from a window, the echo of slaps, the killings of '47, and then, a long separation…

Next day in the afternoon. Amolak, looking out for the marks described by his father, came to the house with the lilac tree. An old, sickly and dejected man lay on a cot under the shade of the lilac. A woman sitting on another cot next to his, was fanning him with a reed fan.

She got up at the knock, calling out—"Who is there?'

Tall with sharp features, large blue eyes, clear fair complexion and a well proportioned body,-fifty-five or sixty years of age, she came up and stood in the door.

"Are you Nafeesa, Bibiji?" The woman was badly shaken by the question.

"No…no…no, son, I…I am Joginder Kaur. Jindro!" With this Nafeesa had uttered the name that had held her captive for at least forty years. But, her voice shook as she said it.

"I have come from Nauru Nangal with a message. This was the address given to me. Forgive me.'

Amolak was about to leave, when tears spilled from the woman's eyes.

"Come in, son…" she said, wiping her tears with the edge of her *chunni*.

"You give me the message, son, I…am the same…I am not to take her name." Her voice had turned into a deep sigh.

"Chacha Fazala has come from Pakistan…of hakims. He wants to meet you. I have come to fetch you."

She was badly shaken. She had clutched the doorjamb to save herself from falling.

"Come in, son!" Suddenly she said, as though she had come back from some other world. "Why are you standing outside? …Come in and sit on that cot." And she had gone up to the old man with tired steps.

"Who is it, Jinder Kaur?' The old man's voice was still full of strength.

"Some boy has come from Nauru Nangal with a message. My brother has come, from Pakistan," she explained in a choked voice.

"Achcha?" The old man was surprised. "What? Your brother? You never mentioned him earlier."

"He is from my village. Brother of my friends. Fazaldin of the hakims." It seemed that Nafeesa and Joginder Kaur were confused. One was eager to meet Fazal, and the other was trying to explain this desire.

The woman had gone in after Amolak had sat down on the cot.

"Aha…I remember…Fazala! Karamdin's son!" The next moment his happiness at having recollected the person, changed into sadness. "Karamdin was an angel. I was the one to have stabbed him the most." And, he had fixed his eyes on Amolak's face.

"You can see, boy, today I am lying here like a heap of mud. At one time I seemed to be flying in the air. I had picked her up with one arm from your village and flung her on my horse. There was no other girl as beautiful as she in a hundred villages around. I had thought I would enjoy her for a few days and then pass her on, but her beauty bewitched me. She also said that you kill me, but don't let me be humiliated and degraded.'

He was silent as the woman's footsteps were heard. After handing Amolak a glass of water she went back.

"She is a good woman. She has been very faithful and has taken great care of me with all her strength! No Jatti can match her.'

Perhaps the old man had found a listener with great difficulty.

"Remember young man..." Suddenly a touch of sadness tinged his narration.

"No one can be happy by hurting another. You can see it from our condition and our home. Of all the things that I looted and filled my home with, only Jinder Kaur has been faithful. I was well-off, but suddenly I became avaricious...I had filled my home with loot during the riots. One can say that the things had to go but much more has gone with them. Our whole life has been spent, yearning to hear the voice of a child. Remember, when a man is blinded by greed like this, even at that time the Supreme Being looks at him..." He closed his eyes for a moment in great humility.

"But what I can't understand is that I was the sinner, but what was her fault?" With this, his thoughts had overwhelmed him. His head shook, and for a few moments, he could not utter a single word.

The woman came back and handed Amolak a glass of tea, and going up to the old man's cot said in a low voice—"If you think fit, may I go?" There was an entreaty in her voice.

"Do go to see him." There was pain, sympathy and also regret in his voice.

The woman returned to the courtyard.

"Now listen... this is a true incident, son," the old man again picked up his narration.

"She was a grand Pathani. She had a child of seven months with her. The Jats all went after her. That bastard...Dhanna Singh said don't fight amongst yourselves. He who kills the child on the wall, can take the woman. The others were taken aback. I snatched the child from the woman's trembling arms, and smashed him against the wall. Oh, ho ho! Even his wail died in his throat..." With this, the skin on the old man's face shrivelled up.

"My son was of the same age when he died...." He turned his shaking neck and hid his face into the dirty pillow, and sobbed bitterly like a child.

Amolak watched him in silence.

"Look son, I am going to die a worm's death," recovering himself he said resignedly and turned his gaze to the nest on the branch of the lilac tree.

"This is a dove's nest. A crow attacks it every day, to drink the eggs. I keep a watch and protect it, son."

With this he lowered his eyes, and said in a low tone—"I will also become a crow after death." And he closed his eyes and sank into deep thought.

"I am going then!"

He opened his eyes with a start when he heard her voice.

"Go Jinder Kaur, go and meet him! First, apologise to Fazal on my behalf. Then, tell him that ever since they left, no wound ever gets healed here." With this he grimaced and flicked the flies off the cloth covering his left leg.

On way to Nauru Nangal, riding behind Amolak on his cycle, Joginder Kaur was slowly turning into Nafeesa. She asked about the village and the family of the cyclist she was riding behind. Then, she talked about Abba's authority, Abba's orchards, her friends and the good times she had lived in, as if her self-imposed silence was broken!

"See how times change! What have I not had to bear! Abba never let me set a foot out of the haveli. We lived in strict purdah! And what degradation I had to face!"

She could not say anything after this. She sobbed to herself rest of the way, continuously wiping her tears.

After meeting Fazal she was so lost in sobs and tears, that for some time no one could say anything.

When Fazal put his hand on her head she wailed.

"See, Vira!" With this she put her head on his shoulder.

"It was the will of Allah."

Fazal supported her and made her sit on the cot.

'Which Allah? Even my Allah has been snatched from me.'

She again broke into sobs. Satta's wife gave her a glass of water, and sitting beside her, tried to console her. She quietened down after some time, began making normal conversation. She asked about Fazal's mother and sisters. Asked about others from the village.

When Fazal asked about her husband, she said—"Even then, he has been good, Vira. He did not humiliate me. He has given me all respect. Now he is bed-ridden. He had a carbuncle on his left leg, and it has gone bad. Nothing should happen to him, brother…" her voice was thick with tears. "Who else do I have except him in this wide world?"

Fazal got up and went in. When he returned he had a box of ointment in his hand.

"Here Nafeesa, apply this on his sore a few times. If you say, I will come and see it myself."

Accepting the box and tying it in a corner of her *chunni*, she said humbly—"Don't be annoyed brother, I have spent forty years trying to be a Jatti among the other Jat women. If you come people would again start digging up the buried past. I would again have to bear taunts from my sisters-in-law and other family members. See my dear brother, how helpless your poor unfortunate sister is," she said sadly.

"I understand everything. Don't you worry, Nafeesa. Amolak will give you more ointment. Nothing will happen to your Sardar." Fazal consoled her.

Nafeesa asked about his wife and children, and asked their names.

"The boys are Dilshad and Bashir, and the daughter is..." he stopped for a moment. "She has your name. Nafeesa." And Fazal bowed his head.

Nafeesa wanted to ask him why he had given her that name, but could not find the words to ask as past memories flooded her mind.

At last she said, "Why did you have to give her that unlucky name?" At this Fazal's eyes had misted, but he made no reply.

When the shadow of the lilac tree touched the edge of the lane which was at some distance, Joginder Kaur, who was still hidden in Nafeesa, thought of her husband, and also the various tasks that had to be done at home. She stood up to leave; Fazal tenderly put his hand on her head, and gave her fifty-one rupees.

"Brother, don't tell anyone that I am alive. It will only dishonour the memory of my dead father."

She sat behind Amolak on his cycle, with tears rolling down her cheeks. She was restless. She had full faith in the ointment tied in a corner of her *chunni*. She herself had once seen the miracle of her abba's wounds being healed by this ointment.

"Sardar will walk in a few days. He will be able to come with me to the gurudwara, morning and evening. Then, after some time he can again take care of the lands himself..." she thought to herself.

When Amolak had dropped her home, her neighbours had asked—"Where are you coming from, Jindero?"

"I had gone to Kuharpur to the gurudwara there." It was Joginder Kaur within Nafeesa who answered, before she hastened into her home.

That evening, Fazal could not decide whether he was happy or sad. But, the question that had troubled him for years had become a heavy burden. The question that had brought him here to this village so that he could find some answers to them.

"Satta, who were they who drove thousands like Santa Singh, Bhag Mal and me away from their birthplaces?" he had asked.

"The British, who else?" Satta had answered quickly.

"No, Satta, no! If the head of the family is wise and strong and the hearts of the members clear, then, no outsider can dare to build a wall in the middle of our courtyared." His voice was steady and strong.

Satta gave no answer to this.

"Satta, what wind had blown which had turned men into something worse than animals?" Again Fazal asked.

Satta made no reply, but Amolak came out of the room, and sat down at the foot of the cot Fazal was sitting on, and remarked -

"Chacha, no one single factor is responsible for what happened."

The old men listened carefully to the young man.

"The greed for more– the lusting after things– this is what drives men to become worse than beasts, Chacha..."

Amolak was silent for a few moments... "Usually man maintains a balance between anger, lust, avarice and arrogance. But the vested interests of the politicians and their propaganda, the religious fanatics all confuse him and finally drives him to bestiality. In times of stress, reason and ideals are abandoned and relegated to our religious texts.

And man shames even animals."

"What is the remedy for this?"

To Fazal Amolak's argument seemed very sensible.

"True interpretation of religion. The educated must play their proper role and be socially more responsible. Total respect should be given to other faiths and beliefs. It must be understood that what hurts us also hurts them. They also mourn their dead. We must accept that they are also like us." Satta was surprised at his own son's beliefs.

"Very good, son! Tell us more..."

At this encouragement from Fazal, Amolak said – "Man should be able to ask questions. He should at least ask 'Why should I kill another?' Chacha, such questions alone can strike at the root of all killing and riots." He was again silent.

"If anyone could only ask the plunderers whether my abba was advisor to Aurengzeb, or Aslam cobbler was a minister of Jahangir, or Meherdin nambardar was a class fellow of Zakaria Khan!" Fazala had thought to himself in those moments.

"It is right, son, but who waits to ask questions and who gives answers when there is a fire raging around you?" Fazal had said in a low tone.

"Chacha, this 'why' must be instilled in the children. It is the duty of parents and teachers to develop the capacity to think and reason. They shouldn't make their children a part of the crowd, but seek to make them conscientious and thinking individuals. If we cannot do this, then unfortunate events like '47 and '84 will happen, time and again. If we take care of our future generations, we can take care of the country, and the world."

This assertion by Amolak lifted the burden that Fazal had been carrying for all these years, and brought him a sense of elation. A surge of pride for the coming generations filled him with hope.

Early next morning Fazal had once again gone to Mian's haveli. His feet stopped at the place from where he had looked at Nafeesa with love, all those years ago.

"Bapuji, come out, Babaji from Pakistan is here."

He raised his eyes to see Santa Singh's granddaughter standing in the window. He had laughed out loud. He did not know why. Was it at what the girl had said, or at the time gone by?

He and Santa Singh had sat talking about various things, till the afternoon.

Then he had gone back to 'his home' and spent the afternoon there. Bhag Mal Jhangi had wept talking about his country that he had left behind. He had met Boota Singh Kler as he had turned towards Satta's home.

"Just see the tricks that fate has played with us! The most beautiful and fertile land has been taken away from us and we have been thrown here on this barren land!"

Fazal could say nothing.

"Someone should ask us how precious this barren piece of land is to us!" He had thought and turned to Satta.

Satta was busy talking to Maddi Brahmin, who had left the village to live in the town, because of deteriorating conditions. He, however, visited the village every fortnight or so. This afternoon he was waiting for Fazal.

"Hindustan a Hindu state! Pakistan a Muslim state!" He had murdered and driven away thousands of Muslims repeating this formula, which had been the basis of the division of the country. He was about seven years older than Fazal. But Fazal could not recognise him. When Satta introduced him, then, Fazal hugged him. But Maddi's arms were stiff, he looked lost and his eyes seemed lifeless.

"How is your Pakistan?" Maddi's harsh tone had jarred on Fazal.

"The same as here, brother. Leaders are busy everywhere misleading innocent people. We are aware of your problems, and our problems are not hidden from you. Our leaders are firmly entrenched in power by depicting our neighbours as fiends."

Maddi had listened to all this, nodding his head in agreement.

"Fazaldin, I feel so helpless, I have had to leave the village and also my people. I have had to leave a fine home here and live in a rented house. Now, it is difficult to even feed oneself. I have had to ask my intelligent son to give up his studies and have put him to work."

Maddi's rough voice expressed his deep sorrow.

Silence had , once again, overtaken them for some ime.

"It is all fate, Panditji. Who could say that this too would happen." Satta remarked sadly.

"At that time, we had also thought that we would gain by sending them away. We murdered the centuries old bonding between the people, by listening to some unknown, unseen people. Today, when we are face to face with the consequences, we now realise how cosy and warm our nests were at that time! Now, I have come to understand the pain of birds who lose their nests, Satta."

Fazal listened to all this in silence.

"Panditji this storm will also blow away after some time. Things will settle down." Satta had consoled Maddi.

"We too had thought the same while leaving the village—God willing, may this storm be shortlived." Fazal had thought to himself. With this thought, he had raised his hands in prayer.

"May you come back to your home as soon as possible. God willing, you may live in your home. May God never let such upheavals occur anywhere in the world."

Listening to Fazal's prayer, Maddi was shaken to the core of his being. Looking at Fazal in astonishment, he had said in a low tone—"What sort of a person are you, you creature of God! We are still steeped in our rites and rituals! But you... you have made us feel very small.., smaller than when we were born, Fazalia!"

No one had responded to this.

He had sat there, looking at the ground for a long time, and then, looking at the setting sun, had got up to leave.

"Panditji, stay with us tonight."

When Satta said this, tears had come to Maddi's eyes.

"I will surely stay, let Fazal's prayer be granted." Saying this he had suddenly spread out his arms to Fazal.

"Come, Fazal, we have both been burnt by the same fire, brother!"

And he had hugged Fazal, pressing him to his chest.

"It is very hard to abandon our homes..." Tears spilled over.

On his way to the bus stop, Maddi was thinking "Religion is not bigger than human beings. Those who harass people, making them homeless, killing them ... can never be religious. I was mad to be proud of killing Muslims, and had gone about arrogantly narrating tales of how cruelly I had treated them. My eyes were opened with the murder of my innocent brother, and I had then thought of my evil deeds, when I was locking up my home. But Fazaldin's prayers have really struck the greatest blow." Sunk in these thoughts he stood at the stop waiting for the bus.

"How trivial my problem is before Fazal's sorrow ... and how small I am compared to him!"

"*O bhagwan* may I reach home safely", he had prayed in his heart while boarding the bus, and cursed the darkness all around, out of an unknown fear.

That night, Fazal had mostly been silent.

"Satta, is Dhanna alive?" He had asked softly.

He is, but just. I saw him at the hospital once. His nephews had brought him in a cart. His body was full of wounds. He had returned from Delhi year before last, after the massacre there.'

"I'll go to see him tomorrow in the morning." Fazala had decided.

Fazal was deeply saddened by what Maddi had said. To rise above all bitterness, he had tried to recall the face of his childhood friend Dhanna. But, Dhanna's betrayal had increased his bitterness.

"There is hope only in future generations now." And, with this thought, his bitterness had abated and he had drifted into sleep.

Next morning, the two friends woke up early and set off on the road to Lahli.

The mud path had now become a tarred road. The roofless *takiya* now seemed a small dump to Fazal. He had closed his eyes and bowed to it, and had thought of the jostling crowds that had always been there in the times gone by. The lights, the offerings, the mimics making the people laugh, the qawwals competing with each other, and Mian Mohammad Baksh showering money on them. Suddenly, the recollection of his father's wounded body had shaken him.

"There was a mango grove here, Satta. How often we had hidden there after bunking school!" Fazal was full of reminiscences as they crossed the stream at Bassi Kalan.

"... Once, a thorn had pierced Dhanna's toe. Even today sitting in Lahore, I tremble when I think of that day. I had flung him on my shoulder and set on the road to the village, as he wept and wailed. Taya had given us both such hard slaps, that I can still feel his hand on my cheek when I think of it. After all, it was a Jat's hand! After that we never missed school! Though we dropped out of school permanently soon after we both failed." And Fazal had laughed at this memory of times gone by.

As soon as they entered the outskirts of Lahli, Fazala had bowed to the earth. Satta could not understand the meaning of this action of his. He watched in astonishment.

Dhanna still lived in the same house but its condition had deteriorated. Satta was about to knock on the door, when Fazal remarked "*Oye*, tell me does one knock on one's own door?"

Both had gone in. A large bedstead stood in the courtyard, and a man, who seemed to be a mere handful of bones, lay on it. Satta stopped at the threshold, but Fazala advanced into the courtyard.

"*Oye* Jatta!" Fazal had put one hand on the bed and enquired—"Why are you still in bed, Singha, like a weakling? Sit up and shout!"

Dhanna did try to straighten his body, but desisted with a groan. He managed to utter—"I have not recognised you?" He looked keenly at the face bending down on him.

"Why would you now recognise a *laagi*, you *dhodar kanva*!" These were the nicknames given to them by their classmates. Fazal was *laagi*—a menial, and Dhanna—a raven crow!

Dhanna recalled some faint memories of his past, but quickly dismissed them with the thought that it was not possible. Even then, a suspicion had arisen in his mind.

"Which village are you from, brother?" He stammered.

"I am from Nauru Nangal. Tell me have you heard the name of this village earlier!" There were both affection and complaint in Fazal's voice.

"What did you say?" There were sudden tears in Dhanna's deep and frightened eyes.

"Oh...Fa...za...lia! You!!"

Fazal also could not restrain his tears. They sobbed for quite some time.

"Stop it, you two, and talk to each other," Satta had tried to intervene.

"This is wonderful!" Dhanna wiped his tears with the edge of his dirty turban.

"I seek your forgiveness, Fazalia. Hit me with your shoes, friend," he had pleaded.

"Stop crying. Now tell me about your home and family," Fazal had said, sitting at the foot of his bed.

"Home? What home? You can see for yourself! My daughter is back home a widow. My son-in-law was a driver, and was killed last year, in Delhi. I saw my eldest son being burnt to death with my own eyes. They put a tyre round his neck and set him on fire. His wife has gone back to her parents. I tried my best to persuade her to marry my younger son, but she didn't agree. And I also cannot complain. He is a no-good, a drug addict..." Dhanna's voice broke under the weight of his worries.

"What about farming?" Fazal had tried his best to divert the conversation.

"One can cultivate if one has lands! The land was all sold long back, Fazal. It has become difficult even to feed ourselves."

Silence had prevailed for some time. Fazal did not have to ask any more questions.

"What should I hide from you! My daughter was of marriageable age. The bastards took her away. She was very beautiful—like her mother. I too had abducted her mother like this, from Dhullial Rathan. My wife passed away only last year. She taunted me till the last day—'Now you would understand the pain of a daughter being abducted.'"

Fazal and Satta had listened to his woes in silence.

"Fazalia, if given an opportunity I'd give my life for you…but what is the use of saying all this now…what we did came back to us in the same way. Even worse! We sowed thorns, what else could we reap?"

Dhanna's daughter had brought water for them. Fazal was upset at the sight of a white dupatta covering her head.

"Deepo, this is your chacha, Fazaldin." The girl had stopped at this. Fazal got up and had put a loving hand on her head—"I and your father were classmates. But he would not have told you about me."

Silence had overwhelmed the sad atmosphere in the courtyard for a long time.

Dhanna's daughter had brought tea for them.

While sipping tea, Fazal's eyes had fallen on the chest lying in a corner of the courtyard. His heart was filled with pain. This was their chest. His mother's dowry chest.

"I was the first woman of the working class to bring a chest in her dowry. It was made of neem wood." Till the end his mother had often talked about this box.

Fazal looked at everything closely. Dhanna, aware of his glance, tried to cover the bare legs of the bedstead with a sheet with the help of his right leg, but his wounded leg was of no use to him. Fazal had read the inscription etched out in nails on the legs of the bed. He had pressed his hand on the inscription surreptitiously, so that Dhanna and Satta may not see him. He wanted to touch the chest also, but thinking of the condition of bedridden Dhanna, he suppressed his desire.

Before leaving he gave Dhanna's daughter fifty-one rupees, and taking a box of ointment from the pocket of his shirt, put it in Dhanna's wounded hand.

"What is this?" Dhanna had asked, deeply moved.

"Ointment," Fazal had answered.

"*Oye*, you are giving me ointment in return for the wounds! What sort of death are you giving me today after half a century! Friend, at least forgive me once!" Dhanna brought his trembling hands together.

"Be happy, Dhanna. I have forgiven you, not once but a thousand times. Now, get well soon and look after your family. Khuda hafiz!" Fazal had said this while hugging Dhanna as he lay on his bed. More than this he could not utter. He walked out, wiping his tears.

Dhanna's sobs had followed them till the end of the lane.

Turning towards the village, Fazal had said—"Satta, you know so many people. Look for a boy from a needy family of Jats. Is there any difference between Dhanna's daughter and our daughter?"

"I'll do that", Satta had said, in all seriousness.

Next morning, Surjan, son of Khairu Lubana, had come with the tonga a little before the appointed time. Half the village was at the door to bid farewell to Fazala. Each one of them had some gift for him.

A stranger made his way through the crowd, and placed a turban in his hands.

"This has been sent by Dhanna Singh of Lahli," he had said with great humility.

Fazal kissed the turban and put it on his head.

"Our honour was one, even earlier, and even now it is one, and may God keep it so till the end of the world." He had thought to himself.

The Sialkotis had asked him to pay obeisance on their behalf to the earth which lay beyond the river Ravi.

Fazal bid farewell to one and all, and then suddenly, he sat down. Lowering his head he kissed the earth of his village. Then, the two friends mounted the tonga. Satta was to see him off at the railway station. Surjan was ready to set off.

"Fellow villagers..." Fazal began and everyone fell silent to listen to him.

"Tell your children about us, the way you relate a grandmother's tale. We have to make them good human beings..." his voice grew heavier with each word.

"May Allah save everyone from further tragedy. May no one be inflicted with wounds. And, if they are, then this ointment would surely heal their wounds. I have given the prescription of this ointment to Amolak. Farewell." And, Fazal wiped his overflowing eyes with the edge of the turban sent by Dhanna.

There was not a single dry eye when Surjan started the tonga and slowly, drove out of sight.

Translation: Tripti Jain

Glossary

Achcha	good; right; well; fine.
Aadaab	salutation; etiquette.
Agha Hashar Kashmiri	a well known Urdu playwright.
Allah Khair	May God be with you.
Amma/Ammi	mother
Amrit	sweetened consecrated water administered in Sikh baptism or initiation.
Asa di war	collection of hymns by Guru Nanak Dev, morning prayers
Babaji	old man; grandfather; term of respect for holy men.
Balle-balle	well done; grand; how grand; expression of happiness.
Bebe/Bebey	grandmother; also used for mother or elder sister.
Benaami	property held in another's name.
Beta	son / child
Beti	daughter
Bhabhi jaan	elder sister-in-law, elder brother's wife
Bhai Saheb	older brother- a mode of address.
Bharai	the drum beaters' caste.
Bibiji / Bijee	term of respect for older women; mother/ sister/ a term of address for daughter / sister / daughter-in-law.
Bohad	banyan tree
Boli	dialect; jibe; sarcasm.
Burqa	a kind of mantle or veil covering the whole body from head to foot.
Chacha	father's younger brother; uncle.
Chaupal	village assembly hall; meeting place.
Chaubara	balcony; an open room on the roof with windows on all sides.

Chitralekha	a movie produced in 1941, based on the novel of the same name (1934) by Bhagwati Charan Verma.
Chowdhery/Chaudhary-	village headman; community leader; prominent person; an honorific term for Jats.
Chulah	earthen hearth
Chunni	light headcloth for women; scarf.
Dadi	grandmother; father's mother
Gilli-danda	a children's game with a wooden stick in place of a ball and a longer stick as a bat
Hakim	physician; especially one practising the Unani system of medicine.
Halwa	an Indian semolina pudding.
Halwai	confectioner; sweetmeat seller.
Haram	forbidden
Heer	the heroine of the legendary romance *Heer-Ranjha*
Haveli	a mansion; a large walled house.
Huzoor	Sir, Your Honour; a term of respect.
Inshallah	God willing.
Janab	Sir; Your Honour, a term of respect
Kachcha	underpants; underwear shorts, one of the five things prescribed for a baptised Sikhs
Kambhakt	unfortunate; wretched.
Kameez/ Kamiz	shirt
Kaptain/Kaptaan	captain
Katori	small bowl or cup
Kavi darbar	a gathering of poets.
Kirpan/kirpan	curved sword carried by baptised Sikhs.
Keertaniya	singer of hymns
Kheer	milk pudding
Khuda Hafiz	may God protect you; farewell.
Krishan Chander	a well known Urdu/Hindi writer.
Kurta	Indian style shirt.
Langar	community kitchens run in Gurudwaras

Main wari Jaawain	an expression of love- 'may I die for you.'
Mallika Pukhraj	a well known classical ghazal singer of the era.
Mar Jaiwain dhiye	'may you die, daughter' used lovingly.
Mataji	mother; a term of address for an old woman.
Mian	a term of respect affixed to Muslim names; father, husband.
Mochi	cobbler; cobblers' caste.
Mohalla	a residential area, an urban district.
Mudda	a reed chair
Nambardar	village head man.
Nayyar O.P.	music director and singer, who later on attained great fame in the sixties and seventies.
Noor Jahan	a famous actress and singer, later on was known as '*Mallika-e-Tarranum*.' (Queen of melody)
Panch	member of a village council known as 'panchayat'
Prabha	a term of respect
Pulao	dish of rice cooked with vegetables/ meat, dry fruits and spices.
Rab/Rabba	God; Oh god.
Ramdulari	an actress and singer of that period, who played a prominent role in the film *Chitralekha*.
Ratan	proper noun, literally meaning jewel. Also the name of a film, a blockbuster starring Swaranlata and Karan Dewan which was made in 1944. It created history with its music, and was the first movie where the music director was given great prominence. The music director was Naushad.
Roshanlal Bhatnagar	a very popular radio singer of the forties and fifties.
Saini	an agricultural caste
Saheb	'Sir'; a term of respect.
Sakrant	the beginning of a month in the sidereal solar calendar considered auspicious.
Sat Sri Akal	the Sikh salutation; Truth (God) is timeless literally the timeless one.
Salaam-uleikam	salutation; peace be with you.
Sheikh	Muslim chief or dignitary.
Sibal	silk-cotton trees

Sunnat	Muslim rite of circum cision.
Taya	father's older brother.
Taiji	his wife
Takiya	Muslim hermitage or monastery.
Tamasha	amusing incident, entertainment
Tehsildar	a revenue officer
Teli	a caste involved in extraction of oil.
Thali	round flat plate or tray with vertically raised edges.
Thanedar	police officer incharge of a police station.
Vidyanath Seth	a well-known radio singer
Upendra Nath 'Ashk'	a famous Urdu/Hindi writer of that period.
Waris Shah	the author of the famous mystical Punjabi romance- *Heer Ranjha* – an integral part of Punjabi culture / literature / psyche.
Water Hindu/Muslim	water sold by Hindu/ Muslim vendors for people of these communities, this was before Independence.
Wuzoo	ablutions for prayers.
Zamindar	landlord; landowner

Our Authors

Ahmed Salim (1945-) is a Pakistani writer and the Policy Advisor for Education and Religious Diversity in the Sustainable Development Institute at Islamabad. A poet, fiction and travelogue writer, he has also written biographies and memoirs. Salim writes in three languages. Punjabi, Urdu and English. His major works are *Naal Mere Koi Chale* (novel), *Titlian te Tank* (novel), *Yaaden Yaaden* (memoir) and *Tantumbar* (poetry). Recipient of several awards, he has recently been honoured by the Ravi Memorial Trust Award for lifetime achievement. A frequent visitor to India, he is particularly sensitive to the commonality we share. The story in this collection is an evidence of that; cultures and histories refuse to be buried or silenced.

Baldev Singh (1942-) is a well known Punjabi writer who has published more than sixty books which include novels, short stories, travelogues, plays and several books for children. He began his career as teacher, first in Muktsar, then moved to Himachal Pradesh, before going on to Calcutta in search of better prospects. 'Come, Sister Fatima' is the story of his mother and her friend Fatima who shared a bond of friendship, a bond that survived in memory and in the spinning wheel. Widely travelled and exposed to several cultures, he is engaged creatively transforming these experiences into his writing.

Gulzar Singh Sandhu (1935-) like many of his contemporary writers has a Masters in English literature, followed by a career in different capacities in the Agricultural University, Ludhiana. His personal memories and experiences of the Partition and his strong association with land pervade all his work. Sandhu has served as editor of the Punjabi *Tribune* and as Chairman of the Punjabi Arts Council. He has several works of fiction to his credit of which *Ek Sanjh Purani* (1965) and *Amar Ratna* (1977) are memorable. 'Gods on Trial' is based on the happenings in the writer's village when forced conversions took place but they were in no way a protection against an act of violence which forced on the villagers a recognition of their own responsibility and led to an active interest in protecting the Muslims. Written in 1956, it was first published in Rajinder Singh Bedi's magazine *Chetna*.

Gurbachan Singh Bhullar (1937-) was born in a village close to Bhatinda. After completing his education, he became a teacher but was soon dismissed on account of his leftist ideology. Later Bhullar took over the editorship of the Punjabi *Tribune*. Despite these frays into different areas, his roots are in a literary life, which he had begun as a poet. His well known works are *Upra Mard, Mein Gaznawi Nahin* and *Agni Kalash*. In 2014 he published his novel *Janam Tumhare Lekhe*. Amongst his many awards are Nanak Singh, Kulwant Singh Virk, Balraj Sahni awards. Gurbachan Singh Bhullar is also the recipient of the Sahitya Akademi and Punjabi Sahitya Akademi Awards.

Gurbaksh Singh Preetlari (1895-1977) a trained engineer who took his training at Roorkee and then at Michigan, Ann Arbor in the States, has a unique status in Punjabi literary studies His travels and political ideas led him to set up a township equidistant between Amritsar and Lahore, named *Preetnagar* (the city of love), where the idea was to locate Punjab's cultural hub. Many major literary figures found their way there—Nanak Singh, Balraj Sahni, Sahir Ludhianvi, Upendra Nath Ashk and several others. The Partition disturbed its development as it formed a border area but it has survived the disruption and has partly revived its original spirit due to the efforts of the family. Gurubaksh Singh wrote poetry, fiction and prose and has more than fifty books to his credit. Some well known titles are *Unwahihi Maa. Bhabhi Maina, Anokhe te Ekale* and an autobiography *Meriyan Apul Yaaden* (My Unforgettable Memories).

Keki N. Daruwalla, poet, novelist and a short story writer has to his credit twelve collections of poetry, five of short stories and two novels. In 1984 he was honoured with the Sahitya Akademi Award for his poetry collection *The Keeper of the Dead* and the Commonwealth Poetry Prize (Asia) in 1987 and a Padma Shri in 2014. Formerly of the IPS, he has served on several important assignments, has travelled extensively in India and abroad and has the knack of capturing the local cultural idiom—an advantage as this allows him to set his work in different locations. 'Black Waters, Dark Well' moves between the two, now divided, territories of the pre-1947 Punjab as well the Delhi-Haryana belt.

Kulwant Singh Virk (1921-1987) is an eminent writer who has captured the rural scenario very graphically in his writing. Born in a village, now in Pakistan, he completed his education in Amritsar and went on to join the Army. During the partition years he worked as a Liaison Officer and the two stories in this collection are about those experiences of those who were to be evacuated. Later he was the editor of the Punjabi magazine *Jagriti* and the English journal *Advance*. Amongst his many awards are the Sahitya Akademi (1969) for *Naven Lok* and the Punjab Council's award in 1981.

Mohinder Singh Sarna (1923-2001) novelist, short story writer and poet has several collections of short stories and novels to his credit. His long poem *Chamkor* won him the Bhai Santosh Singh Award (1974). Among his other awards are the Sahitya Akademi (1994) and the Punjab Government's Shromani Sahitkar Award (1989). His contribution to the novel has been the penetrating psychological insight into human relations. The two stories published in this collection are based on personal experiences, largely autobiographical and connected with his own migration from Rawalpindi. 'A Defender of Humanity' appeared in his collection *Kala Badal, Kooleec Dhup* (Dark Cloud, Soothing Sunlight). Sarna served in the Indian Audit and Accounts Service.

Navtej Singh (1925-1981) was born in Sialkot in a family which has established itself as a leading literary family in Punjab. He graduated in psychology and the impact of this training is evident in his work. Enthused with communist ideas almost all his writing reflects upon socio-economic issues. He wrote a regular column titled 'Meri Dharti, Mere Lok'. Some of his major works are *Desh Wapsi*, *Basmati di Mehak*, *Channan De Beej*. In 1977 he took over the editorship of *Preetlari*. Navtej died young at fifty six, but the literary legacy has been passed on to the third generation and *Preetlari* is one of the rare journals that has survived the partition. 'Homecoming' is the title story of the collection of *Desh Wapsi*. Apparently based on a newspaper report, according to his daughter-in-law Poonam Singh, it captures the coming together of contrary emotions at a moment of national rupture. The Panjabi Vibhag conferred on him the award of Shiromani Patrakar in 1977, in recognition of his literary contribution to journalism by creating a new form combining the style of article writing and story writing ('Varta' and 'Kahani').

Prem Parkash (1932-) has combined several interests—farming, teaching and writing. A Masters in Urdu, he had worked in daily newspapers and *Lakeer* magazine in editorial capacities. He has written several novels and short stories. In addition he also has four autobiographical works. Recently the writer has put together his stories on the militancy years 1980-1992 under the title *Aswathama de Mathe da Zakhm* (The Wound on Aswathama's Forehead). Amongst his several awards are the Sahitya Akademi (1992), Punjabi Academy, Delhi (1996), Shiromani Punjabi Sahitkar Sanman (2002) and Punjabi Sahit Ratan Award (2011).

Sanwal Dhami (1968-) is a pseudonym that Dhami has adopted, his given name being Charn Pushpinder Singh. He belongs to the village Singriwala in Hoshiarpur District, where he continues to live and teach. He has to his credit several works which include poetry, fiction and criticism. Dhami has several other stories about the Partition and its aftermath. 'The Ointment' carrying the title 'Malham' in the Punjabi original, is a story born out of his sensitivity to the aftermath of the Partition and the awareness the similarity in the experiences of violence and the suffering on both sides. The story carries the message of reaching across to the other—the only way to avoid a replay of gruesome events, and marks the nostalgic shift in memory.

Surjit Sarna writes both poetry and fiction and has also contributed to a three part play *Kafle* besides writing a biographical memoir. Her strengths lie in the sensitive portrayal of emotion and her ability to capture a small moment to enter into a wider psychological probing. Sarna's major works are *Nagma Patjhar Da*, *Gal Mere Ishq Di*, *Lahore Kini Dur* and *Vichore Ban Gaye Sadiyan*. She has also worked as a freelance newsreader for AIR and has translated several novels for the Sahitya Akademi. Many of her short stories were first published in magazines and newspapers. 'Lahore Kini Dur' translated as 'The Distance to Lahore' is from her collection of the same title, while 'Nargis de Phul' translated as 'A Bunch of Narcissus' was first published in the Punjabi *Tribune* in 1996. She is the recipient of the Sahitya Akademi Award for translation.

Tahira Iqbal lives in Faislabad, Pakistan, where she is Professor of Urdu. Born in a village, she hails from a conservative family and was mostly educated at home. Dr. Iqbal has four collections of short stories, the latest of these was chosen the Best Work for 2014. She also writes novellas, travelogues and academic papers, besides writing columns for newspapers and magazines. The village to which she belongs had a large population of refugees from East Punjab, who, despite the hardships they had experienced, grew to think differently of their erstwhile homeland and its people. Tahira says, "They tried to compare the fruits, vegetables, weather and even the quality of the air…their mind was still trapped in the past." I first heard her read 'One's Own Country' at a SAARC conference in Delhi.

Our Translators

Hina Nandrajog has done her doctoral thesis from Punjabi University, Patiala and is an Associate Professor at Vivekanand College. A scholar and a translator, she has published several critical articles and translates both from Punjabi and Hindi into English. She has won several awards. Among them are the Katha Translation Prize in 1999 and 2001, and the Sahitya Akademi, Consolation Translation Prize in 2008. She has been part of several translation projects of the National Book Trust, Centre for Development of Punjabi Language and Culture, Patiala and the Punjabi Academy Delhi. Three stories in this volume: 'Fattu the Bard', 'Come Sister Fatima' and 'You Will Always Be My World,' have been translated by her.

Jasbir Jain is a critic and a columnist. Formerly Professor of English at the University of Rajasthan, she has translated articles from Hindi and short stories from Punjabi, in addition to a collaborative translation of Hansa Wadkar's Marathi autobiography *Sangtye Aika*, published by Zubaan, under the title *You Ask, I Tell*. Jain's literary interests are wide-ranging and include drama, gender issues, culture and ideology. Her contribution to this volume is the translation of Surjit Sarna's, 'Lahore Kini Dur.'

Madhuri Chawla is an Associate Professor at Dyal Singh Evening College, where she teaches English. She translates from Punjabi to English. Her translations have been published in several literary journals which include *Indian Literature, Creative Forum, Journal of Literary and Critical Writings, Journal of Aesthetics and The Little Magazine* among others. Madhuri has reviewed and subedited several books and is a freelance writers for the *Hindustan Times*. She has translated several partition stories for the volume *Santalinama* for the Punjabi Academy, New Delhi. Prem Parkash's story 'Without a Homeland' is one of those translation.

Navtej Sarna is an Indian diplomat and a writer of novels, short stories, essays and a translator. He has authored *The Exile, We Weren't Lovers Like That, Winter Evenings* and his non-fiction works are *The Book of Nanak* and *Folk Tales of Poland*. His major translations are *Zafarnama* and *Savage Harvest*. Navtej's short stories have been broadcast on BBC World Service and he is a regular contributor of *The Hindu, The Times Literary Supplement* and several other journals and magazines. Presently he is posted as India's ambassador to the United States.

Raj Gill (1931-99), a blingual writer, wrote both in English and Punjabi. Some of his works are *Parchawaan, Tasveer, Channan di kut*. In English he has several novels and critical works of which *The Golden Dawn, The Rape* and *Patterns of Survival* are noteworthy. Sensitive and responsive to the world around him, he always maintained a mini zoo at home. This volume carries his translation of Gulzar Singh Sandhu's story 'Gods on Trial'.

Tripti Jain, trained as a political scientist, brings a rare sensitivity to literature. Recipient of the Katha South Asian Translation Award, 2002, for her Punjabi translation, she translates both from Punjabi and Hindi into English as well as from English into Hindi. Her translations include several full-length novels, short stories and critical essays which have been published in anthologies and journals. Her work has been published by Oxford University Press, Sahitya Akadimi, National Book Trust and Sage/Rawat. For the present volume, she has translated 'The Homecoming', 'Danghter's Dowry', 'Khabal/Perennial Grass', 'One's Own Country'and 'The Ointment'.

Acknowledgements

The editors gratefully acknowledge the permission given by the writers and the translators to include the following copyright material in the present anthology.

Navtej Singh's heirs for 'The Homecoming', Mohinder Singh Sarna's heirs for 'Of One Community' and 'A Defender of Humanity', Kulwant Singh Virk's family for 'Daughter's Dowry' and 'Perennial Grass' (Khabal), Gulzar Singh Sandhu for 'God's on Trial', Gurbachan Singh Bhullar for 'Fattu the Bard', Prem Parkash for 'Without a Homeland', the Preetlari family for Gurbaksh Singh Preetlari's 'You Will Always Be My World', Surjit Sarna for 'The Distance to Lahore' and 'A Bunch of Narcissus', Baldev Singh for 'Come, Sister Fatima', Ahmed Salim for 'The Man who Refused to Die', Keki N. Daruwala for 'Black Waters, Dark Well', Tahira Iqbal for 'One's Own Country', Sanwal Dhami for 'The Ointment'.Our sindere thanks to the translators—Tripti Jain, Navtej Sarna, Raj Gill's heirs, Hina Nandrajog, Madhuri Chawla, Ahmed Salim and Jasbr Jain for their translations and permission to use their translations.

We also thank the first publishers of the work included in this collection: 'Homecoming' was published in *Azadi De Baad Diyan Kahaniyan* (National Book Trust), 'A Defender of Humanity' and 'Of One Community' (the family), these stories are included in *Savage Harvest* (Rupa). 'Daughter's Dowry' and 'Khabal/Perennial Grass' are from *Meriyan Sariyan Kahaniyian,* (Navyug), 'Gods on Trial' (Orient Paperbacks), 'Without a Homeland', 'Fattu The Bard', 'Come, Sister Fatima' and 'You will Always be My World' from *Santalinama: Partition Stories* (Punjabi Akademy, Delhi), Keki N. Daruwalla, the author, Ahmed Salim the author, Surjit Sarna's stories *The Tribune* (Punjabi) Tahira Iqbal. 'One's Own Country' original from the volume *Rekhat* (Dost Publications), Sanwal Dhami for 'Ointment' from *Malham Ate Hor Kahaniyan* (Punjabi, Chetna Prakashan).

In addition to the above, several friends have helped us in this endeavour. We acknowledge the help given by the writers themselves, all of whom generously gave of their time and Tejwant Singh Gill, Sukhdev Singh, Navtej Sarna, Nirupama Dutt, Mini Krishnan, Gulzar Singh Sandhu and Tahira Iqbal, all of who went out of their way to extend help. Our special thanks and gratitude to Mini Krishnan for her advice and her valuable review of the translations.

Finally, we thank Shri Bikash Niyogi and Smt Tultul Niyogi of Niyogi Books—our present publishers. And to Mohua Mitra, the editor of the volume.